A Beautiful Offering

Other Books from Angela Thomas

When Wallflowers Dance

Do You Think I'm Beautiful?

Do You Think I'm Beautiful? Bible Study and Journal

Tender Mercy for a Mother's Soul

Prayers for the Mother to Be

An Expectant Mother's Journal

Prayers for New Mothers

A Beautiful Offering

Returning God's Love with Your Life

Angela Thomas

Thomas Nelson
Since 1798

NASHVILLE   DALLAS   MEXICO CITY   RIO DE JANEIRO

Published in Nashville, Tennessee, by Thomas Nelson. Thomas Nelson is a registered trademark of Thomas Nelson, Inc.

Published in association with Nelson Books and Creative Trust, Inc., Literary Division, 2105 Elliston Place, Nashville, TN 37203.

Thomas Nelson, Inc., titles may be purchased in bulk for educational, business, fund-raising, or sales promotional use. For information, please e-mail SpecialMarkets@ThomasNelson.com.

ISBN 978-0-7852-8826-8 (trade paper)

Library of Congress Cataloging-in-Publication Data

Thomas, Angela, 1962-
    A beautiful offering : returning God's love with your life / Angela Thomas.
      p. cm.
    ISBN 978-0-7852-6357-9 (hardcover)
    1. Christian women—Religious life. 2. Beatitudes. I. Title.
BV4527.T467 2004
248.8'43—dc22   2004001713

Printed in the United States of America

10 11 12 QG 12 11 10

For

Novie Thomas,

with all my love.

Mama, maybe more than anyone I've ever known,

your life is a beautiful offering to God.

Contents

Contents

PART 1

WHEN YOU ARE

~⁀~

MY LAST BOOK, *DO YOU THINK I'M BEAUTIFUL?*, CAME FROM my heart's desire to know the personal and passionate love of God. More than anything, I longed to hear what God had to say of me. I wanted to know if He saw all of me and loved me still. The answer I heard came like a shout from heaven, when God said to me and to you, "The King is enthralled with your beauty."

Both my heart and mind have been overwhelmed by the truth and power of God's intimate, pursuing, rescuing love. And from that gratefulness the question to God that builds in my soul is, How can I return Your love with my life? I truly want my life, these very short years, to become a sweet offering to my Father, the One who invited a girl like me to dance in His arms.

I want to know how my life, this imperfect journey with blemishes and scars, can reflect back to God my gratefulness for His love to me. And so, I have turned to Jesus for instruction. *Show me how to live a life that is beautiful to God. Teach me what He calls pleasing and blessed.* I want to work my way through Jesus' teaching in the Sermon on the Mount and return to Him a passionate pursuit. I want to know what this woman will look like

1

as these truths continue to take deeper hold of me, transforming my heart and life.

It is a privilege to have you come with me. We'll begin with Jesus' words called the Beatitudes. For so many years, I have heard the Beatitudes taught as a list of "Gotta Be's." It seemed as if I always came up short when I stood my life next to the Gotta Be's. I could never seem to reconcile the perceived call to mourning, meekness, and persecution with the rest of Scripture's call to joy, boldness, and strength. It seemed as though the Beatitudes were preached like you *gotta be* all of those things at once. I couldn't figure out how in the world I could be poor and mourning and meek, hungry and merciful and pure, peaceful and persecuted, all in the same woman, all at the same time.

Because of God's new mercy to me, I have loosely begun to call this listing the "When You Are's." That *when you are* poor in spirit, the kingdom of heaven can still be very close. That *when you are* meek, there is even then a spiritual inheritance. That *when you are* merciful, there is more mercy given. We have to stay true to the intent of Jesus, and I believe that in this part of the sermon, He intends for us to learn to respond like Him through these blessings. Some of the blessings come to us when we find ourselves in certain circumstances like poverty of spirit or persecution. And then sometimes the blessing comes because we are becoming spiritually mature as with the pure in heart and the peacemakers.

The kingdom of heaven is the promise that bookends the When You Are's. Essentially Jesus wants us to learn to live in a way that reflects the kingdom of God to the world, to live as a woman with a kingdom heart. I truly want to be that woman. And Jesus says that *when you are*, it's beautiful and blessed.

I guess I always thought that my offering to God had to be perfect and without any flaw, something like a perfect sacrifice. I am coming to understand that the Father receives the offering of my life, even when it is broken or weak or marred. It's the covering of Christ that makes it perfect, and the desire to give my life to God that makes it beautiful.

The more I walk with God, the more I come to know Him as a mystery. Maturing is a journey. We know only in part and usually learn in little lessons. My prayer is that the stories in these chapters will be lessons that inspire your faith and challenge you to move closer and closer to God. May you hear the voice of God call you beautiful. And may you desire with all your heart to return the love of God with your life.

1

BROKEN

⌒

Blessed are the poor in spirit,
  for theirs is the kingdom of heaven. (Matthew 5:3)

The LORD is close to the brokenhearted
  and saves those who are crushed in spirit. (Psalm 34:18)

WHEN I WAS A LITTLE GIRL IN NORTH CAROLINA DREAMING about what I wanted to be when I grew up, I chose the most radical, adventurous, outside-my-box, scare-my-parents-silly thing I could think of. My mom was a nurse and my dad sold produce. I was their firstborn, and I decided that I wanted to be an astronaut. Of course no one took me seriously for a while, which made me all the more determined.

Folks would come over for dinner and I'd hear them talking to my parents. Actually, I was eavesdropping. I'd lurk around the grown-ups, careful not to draw too much attention to myself, silently gathering information. For some reason, I thought that I belonged in their conversation more than I belonged outside on the swing set. I'd overhear one of my parents say, "Angela wants to be an astronaut," and then I'd watch as the guest would look over at me, amazed. I assumed they were thinking, *That squirrelly little four-eyed kid? She seems kind of nerdy, but she must have spunk. She's got big dreams.* I'd puff up on the inside, thinking to myself, *One of these days you are going to watch me land on the moon.*

I kept talking about being an astronaut and reading books on NASA and lunar landings. In the third grade, I sat riveted to watch all the *Apollo* coverage on our grainy black-and-white television. While the other girls were doing book reports on cats or manners, I always chose topics such as space and moon rocks and exploration. I would stir up a glass of Tang for breakfast and think about what it would be like to drink it through a straw while floating upside down in a space suit. We built model rockets at school once, and I was thrilled to get out of that stupid sewing module and onto my life's calling. I knew I'd eventually prove to all the naysayers that I was serious. I didn't know you needed to be a genius to be an astronaut; I thought you just had to want to. And if it was about "want to," then I had it.

One Christmas I asked for and received a telescope so that I could keep an eye on things and chart my course through the stars. Never mind that it was the dinkiest little tabletop telescope ever, with three wobbly legs. I took it outside at dusk and stared at the moon. Soon I had convinced all the neighborhood kids that I could see the United States flag Neil Armstrong and Buzz Aldrin had planted on the lunar surface during the *Apollo 11* mission. I was so sure that I even convinced myself I could see it. I can still remember blurry images of red, white, and blue and my big-shot attitude. "If you were astronaut material, you'd be able to see the flag," I'd argue.

I think that right this very moment is the first time I am consciously realizing that I probably did not actually see the Stars and Stripes from my front yard. This is a hard revelation. But how could you see a flag on the moon with a couple of scratched-up lenses inside a white plastic tube? I guess you can't. How embarrassing. I haven't thought about this in forever, and it's kind of painful to realize I've believed my own hype all these years. A grand imagination dies a bitter, slow death, you know.

I bet you've already guessed where this story is going. One day some know-it-all said, "You can't be an astronaut. Astronauts need perfect vision. You can't wear glasses when you blast off in a rocket. They don't stay on in zero gravity." I'd never heard of such a thing. Then I checked around, and sure enough, back then, it was true. There were no four-eyed astronauts.

How could my best idea for an awe-inspiring, adventurous life be instantly gone? What was I going to do? The big dream inside this skinny girl was shattered. That dream had made me important. Everybody thought I had courage. How was I going to be somebody with no wild, over-the-top career to aspire to?

It was a very difficult day when my astronaut dream broke.

The Jesus Girl

Fast-forward about ten years, and that same nerdy girl meets Jesus in college. Thankfully there were no vision requirements except spiritual eyes to see. Maybe for the first time since the astronaut dream died, I had a reason to live. But I was still me, and I brought my energetic, wait-till-you-see-what-I can-do-for-Jesus attitude to our relationship.

I thought it would work out great. Jesus needed me to show everybody how to be a model, happy Christian, and I needed something to do with my life, since I wouldn't be going to the moon.

I really fell in love with God and jumped into my new reason to live with both of my busy feet. It's like I went from place to place, begging anybody to show me what to do. I was a wild woman. Reading the Bible, doing two or three studies at a time. Praying for hours. Going to church every day I could find one open. Asking anyone who stood still long enough, "If you died tonight, do you know where you'd spend eternity?" I was a quick learner. Just give me the instructions, tell me what the rules are, then stand back and watch. I was going to be the best little Christian girl Jesus ever had.

And you know that whole thing kind of worked for a while. I am predisposed toward happy. I like happy people, and I like to make people happy. So my being happy for Jesus was a good fit. It gave me energy. It propelled me through seminary and the first years of my ministry. It was almost as if nothing could hurt me in those days. I'm sure I was oblivious to the hurt I caused with my happy pride about my happy life, but I was just zinging along, from campfire to campfire, singing,

> I'll shout it from the mountaintops (Praise God!),
> I want my world to know,
> the Lord of Love
> has come to me,
> I want to pass it on.

Well I kept shouting from the mountaintops, wondering why everyone couldn't just find a spark, get a fire going, pass it on, and we'd all snuggle up together beside the warm glowing.

I had wanted the world to know about Jesus and the happy life they could have in Him. What I didn't realize was that life out there in the real world was eventually going to roll in and teach me a thing or two about happy. Make that roll right over on top of me. No, more like put me under an asphalt paver and squish me flat like a bug, you know, where the guts are everywhere and you can't even tell what it used to be? Yep, that's about how it was somewhere around my early thirties.

I love that God gave me a happy-camper life for a while. Some of my best memories were made over s'mores or passing LifeSavers around a room with a toothpick between your teeth. The best stuff happened at a cabin in the woods, or at a sunrise service on the beach, or while tubing down a river with a bunch of crazy friends. The spiritual foundation that God built in those years is priceless to me now.

But when you're running along being the happy-camper Christian girl and you begin to feel your life come apart, it catches you by surprise. Maybe as the happy Jesus girl, I had all the right motives and exactly the right approach for those years, but I was blissfully ignorant about the pain and disappointment that can come to each of us. Before I really knew what was happening, parts of my life began to crack and little pieces started to break off and smash flat. Back then I did the only thing I knew to do: I sang louder and prayed harder and went to more Bible stuff. And that seemed to be the answer until I began to come apart in big chunks and I was singing as loud as I could and the mountaintop was leveled anyway.

It was an even more difficult day when my perfect-Jesus-girl dream broke.

When a Person Breaks

When life is overwhelming and the burdens become more than one human being can bear . . . When your circumstances are unrelenting, or the consequences that have come to you heap higher and higher . . . When tragedy sneaks into your life to ambush you like a stalker, or the world bangs down the door and says, "Let me teach you a few lessons" . . . When there is just too much and you almost can't breathe . . . then people break. Hearts break and the will is broken and dreams shatter and the spirit is crushed.

For some reason I had believed there would be a progression. I'd bring my strengths to Jesus, He'd add more strength, then I'd just get better and better. I used to think that by now I'd probably be a spiritual giant. I guess I thought that after I'd spent most of my life knowing Jesus, I'd outgrow my humanity. I'd outrun the world. I'd rise above and never stumble. I don't know where all these dumb ideas came from, but I was just wrong and strong-willed and insensitive. Did I say the whole sing-louder-to-drown-out-the-heartache thing was dumb? 'Cause if I didn't, it was.

Brokenness comes to us for so many different reasons. Sometimes it's the way the world comes up to greet us. Sometimes it's the consequences of our sin. Sometimes it's the result of a lifetime of poor choices. And then sometimes we can't even untangle the mess to give it a name. Christians break for all the same reasons anybody breaks, because they are human and fragile and prone to wander.

> *I guess I thought that after I'd spent most of my life knowing Jesus, I'd outgrow my humanity.*

I have friends who have been broken by sickness, the death of a child or a spouse, bankruptcy, abuse, rape, addictions, abortion, and on and on. They are Christians who've been crushed in one way or another by tragedy or choices or sin. You know sometimes it starts small and then gets bigger. That's how brokenness came to me. I have been broken by circumstances and choices and then, finally, divorce.

Sometimes we have to use words to describe ourselves that were never meant to be in anyone's vocabulary. We suddenly have words attached to our lives such as *cancer, divorce, rape,* or *widow.*

Sometimes we look around us and know that it's not how we dreamed it, but here it is, and it's all in a million pieces.

It seems like almost every strong believer I know has been broken or remains in broken places. A pastor said to me the other day, "Angela, I don't really trust anyone in ministry who's never been broken." His words were meant as grace to me, and they could not have been more soothing. He gets it. None of us ever went looking for brokenness, but it came to find us anyway, with all its intense lessons on pain and heartache and suffering.

Maybe you've never known anything so painful that it emptied your spirit. Or maybe it seems like you've lived your whole life in pain. Either way, the reality is that it's coming. One way or another, brokenness comes to us all. I'd kind of thought I could skip past it if I kept singing. But Jesus never preached the insulated gospel. That was my own misinterpretation of Him.

Did you ever think the same kinds of things I did? Did you ever believe that being a Christian meant eventually overcoming weakness or reaching a pinnacle of near-perfection on this earth? We can become more mature as believers. We can be made complete for the purposes of Christ on this earth. But until heaven, we cannot escape our humanity and the frailties that come with it. Did you ever think that if you subscribed to a certain set of behaviors, you'd be protected from the effects of living in a fallen world? I don't know if I consciously ever said those things, but as I look back, those kinds of ideas seemed to fuel my actions and attitudes.

The broken person can pick up one of the little pieces lying around, but can't find another one to match. It becomes obvious that this life isn't going to be put back together like a puzzle. Somebody is going to have to start over. But the person who is broken doesn't have the will anymore. The broken person is emptied of desire and dreams and courage. When life breaks and the pieces are crushed, then the spirit of that person becomes desperate and poor.

Poor in Spirit

During all those happy-camper years, I had read about the poor in spirit, but for the life of me I couldn't figure out who in the world Jesus was talking about—certainly not anyone who knew Him as Savior. And then one day it was me. I knew Him as my Savior and Lord, yet there I was—divorced, broken, and mentally, emotionally, and spiritually flattened. I realized that I needed to hear whatever He had to say about being poor in spirit.

When Jesus climbed the hillside one afternoon to give His followers living instructions, He knew they were a bunch of people just like me and you. Maybe they had been singing a rousing chorus of "Pass It On" around a bonfire, squeezed one another's hand, and with a tear of joy, whispered to their neighbor, "God loves you." Maybe some of the more extroverted followers had shimmied up a tree and led a pep rally for Jesus. All together now,

> I am a C.
> I am a C-H.
> I am a C-H-R-I-S-T-I-A-N.
> And I have C-H-R-I-S-T
>   in my H-E-A-R-T
>   and I will L-I-V-E, E-T-E-R-N-A-L-L-Y.

Louder and louder their voices rose. Singing and chanting and laughing and loving one another and their Lord. I would have totally loved it.

Jesus had been healing the sick and casting out demons. People had heard about Him and had come from as far away as Syria to have their loved ones healed. There were crowds from Galilee, Jerusalem, Judea, and from all across the Jordan region. These people were in the presence of the Son of God. Pain was fleeing. Demons were running. The crippled were walking. If there ever had been a reason to sing and shout and dance over Jesus' power and mercy, this had to be the best.

Build bigger bonfires. Bring in more guitars. Sing louder. Throw the stick of your sin into the fire. Hold hands and raise them to the sky. Jesus is Lord. He is Love. He is a Healer. He is more than amazing.

The crowd just kept building, and I am imagining that they were a bunch of happy campers with all this healing and good news going on. These people had heard about the Son of God, just seen the proof of His power with their own eyes, and now Jesus was going to teach them about the possibility of living a life that would be pleasing to God.

Finally, the Savior was among them, and He was going to speak to them from a hillside so that they could see Him. Maybe Jesus had to get the disciples to settle down the newly healed in the back who had just divided their section into three parts and were singing in rounds about "bubblin' over." Maybe they had to tell the demon *un*-possessed to hang on a minute, that testimonial time was slated for a little later in the day. Maybe the disciples kept saying to the people, "We know you're excited, but simmer down—Jesus has something to say to us." Maybe in the presence of these miracles, even the brokenhearted forgot about their pain for a while and leaned in a little closer to hear what this Man had to say.

And then the Reason for all the celebration stood and turned to this exuberant crowd and said,

Blessed are the poor in spirit, for theirs is the kingdom of heaven.

"Huh?" one celebrant leans over and whispers to the next. "What did He just say? I've still got 'Kum Ba Ya' going round in my head, and I'm not sure I heard Him right."

"He said, 'Blessed are the poor in spirit.'"

"Oh. Wonder why He said that. Look at us. We're all so happy. There is a party going on everywhere this Man goes. I'll probably be happy for the rest of my life. My pain is gone, and my daughter can walk for the first time. I think I'll sign up to be on the worship team. Who could possibly be poor in spirit after they meet Jesus?"

"Maybe He knows something we don't, and maybe you should stop humming long enough to listen."

Jesus is amazing. If I had been Him, I would have probably stood to take a bow for all the great healing I'd been doing. Maybe I'd have let the people sing a few rousing choruses to celebrate my goodness. I'm sure I would have said, "Thanks for coming. Wait till you see what I can do next." But Jesus did what no one expected; He began to teach about the character He desires for us—how we can return His love with the offering of our lives. His first lesson reveals the depth of His tender heart when He begins with the poverty of our spirit.

Jesus knew everything we couldn't, and from His compassion He said, first thing, that when you are poor in spirit, when you are broken, when you are completely empty and without one resource—especially then you are blessed. At the very beginning of these life instructions, Jesus let us know that our lives don't have to always be an over-the-top perfected effort. We won't always be singing "I've got the joy, joy, joy, joy down in my heart." How gently He teaches that even in our brokenness, this life can become a beautiful offering to God.

A Beautiful Offering

Did you know that *blessed* means "happy"? How cool is that? It also means "fortunate" or "favored." Probably everyone who had come to listen to Jesus that day was in a pretty festive mood, and obviously He knew that. Instead of bringing them down, He spoke into their celebration. He let them know that life will keep coming with all its heartache and pain. It's not always going to be one big pep rally, but if you are following Christ, if you have become His disciple, then you can still know a happiness that is given by God.

He began His sermon to the healed and free and curious with the When You Are's that we've come to know as the Beatitudes. The word *beatitude* is taken from the Latin word *beatitudo*. And our word *beautiful* is also derived from the same root. I'm going to take a little latitude with the translation here and give you my paraphrase. Maybe it would be all right with Jesus if we said,

Your life is a beautiful offering to God, even when you are poor in spirit, because then you are very close to the kingdom of heaven.

Maybe through the sermon of Jesus, God wants you and me to know that He gets it. He understands humanity, and He's not mad at us about it. He designed the vessel that we reside in. He knows that we get weary. Our muscles fatigue. Emotions fray. Health fails. He wired us to long for the love of one another and without human-being love, He knows there can be desperate loneliness. He completely sees and hears and understands how the spirit can become emptied and broken. And from His understanding comes His compassionate blessing.

If the blessing of being closer to heaven comes through poverty of spirit, then maybe we can come to embrace our brokenness, knowing that we will experience a nearness of heaven that we could not know otherwise. As a woman who longs after God, we can look into our emptiness, trusting that God is drawing us to Himself through life's pain and disappointment.

Very Close to the Kingdom

I am a work-at-home mom. I have four children, two girls and two boys who, at this writing, are ages five to thirteen. They think that I stare at a computer and somehow books appear. Most of the time, I try to write when they are in school because otherwise the rest of our day is just like yours—it can be wild.

Forget the afternoons when everyone has a ball game on a different field at the same time. It's still wacky when we're all at home. I mean, we can be here in the house, even in the same room, with five different things going on. I might be braiding AnnaGrace's hair while she is dressing her Bitty Baby. William would usually be in trouble for throwing something or eating Popsicles on the carpet, Grayson might be sorting his baseball cards or memorizing the presidents in order (Good grief, where did he come from?), and Taylor would invariably be on the phone. We'd all be together in our little kingdom. And yet we each would be distracted by our tasks or goals or just the annoying way the person next to us chews gum.

The other day, William had sinus surgery. I expected it to be a breeze because everyone at the hospital was so nice and smiled at us a lot. The surgery went fine, but the recovery room was a different story. When the nurse called me back, my little seven-year-old was trembling with chills, crying, and bleeding all over the place. For the next few hours, they kept managing his pain, and I kept wiping away tears, his and mine. All the other children were in the waiting room, bored and antsy until they heard their brother cry. Then they sat quietly, realizing that someone they didn't know they loved so much was hurting.

That night after we got an exhausted William home, I loved watching the others care for him while he lay on the couch. Finally it was time for bed. Everything was done or left undone. Baths were taken. Toys put away, sort of. TV off. The phone unanswered. I carried William up to my bed and held him while the others piled on with us. We just lay there snuggled under a blanket for a while. Worn out from the day. Empty and yet peaceful. No one fussing because somebody's toe accidentally touched their pajamas. We remembered that we were a family. On my bed that night, given-out and tired, we were as close to the kingdom of us as it gets.

All the time, you and I are operating inside the kingdom of God. Every moment we have been held by His gaze. He has forever been as close as the beat of your heart and the inclination of your prayer. But sometimes goals and tasks and the annoying way the world rolls in can keep us from realizing His nearness. We forget that we are in His family. We forget that we belong to His kingdom.

The Inheritance

My relationship with Jesus began with my dreaming of becoming a mature, faithful follower. I wanted to shine so brightly that God would really be proud of me. So I set the bar unattainably high and began to structure my life around the dream of being a perfect Jesus girl. I look back now and shake my head. Not in regret, but I do wince at my lack of understanding. I did not understand the heart of God. I didn't realize that forgiveness would be an ongoing process for this earthly pilgrim. I didn't know it was okay to acknowledge emptiness in your spirit. I didn't think that brokenness was acceptable to God. So I learned to pretend for my own sake, and I thought I was pretending to please God.

I know it sounds ridiculous now, but I was truly just doing all I knew. I had no idea about the blessings attached to the When You Are's. I didn't understand that God could look on my imperfection and offer His tender compassion and blessing anyway. It has transformed my entire relationship with God to be able to come to Him *as is,* completely human, worn out, with hurt feelings, procrastinating or aimless. Through prayer I have learned to lay my empty spirit on His altar.

My brokenness is a beautiful offering to Him, and just the act of giving my poor spirit to the Father ushers me into the inheritance of His kingdom. Do you remember the inheritance that is set aside for us? It contains the gifts we could not buy for ourselves—forgiveness, divine comfort, grace, mercy, healing, restoration—all the riches that belong to God, given to us just because we belong to Him.

I feel as though I say this all the time, but God is truly amazing. There is a kingdom inheritance awaiting you and me, and we don't have to be perfect Jesus girls to receive it. Maybe most of my life, anxiety has come from not feeling that I am worthy, but I am supposed to get myself worthy before I can receive a blessing from God. It's almost as if Jesus says, "I know about your brokenness and your flaws. I know that you aren't worthy. That's where I come in. What's Mine is yours anyway."

Jesus wants you to know that when you are broken, shivering, alone, or afraid, with nothing left and nowhere to go, then you can turn in His direction and lay yourself at the foot of His love. Lay your broken offering on His altar. He will come and carry you into His presence. He will hold you with the warmth of His embrace and cover you with the blanket of His kingdom inheritance.

God wants you to know that when everything else is gone, that makes more room for Him, and every time there is more room for Him, you are blessed. He came for all of us, the demon-possessed of Syria, rule keepers from Jerusalem, little girls with astronaut dreams in the South, and happy campers holding hands around bonfires all over the world. He wants you to know that He doesn't mind broken things or broken hearts or broken people. In fact, He dearly loves them.

It's such amazingly good news that you might want to pass it on.

> *God wants you to know that when everything else is gone, that makes more room for Him, and every time there is more room for Him, you are blessed.*

Questions for Reflection and Discussion

⌒

1. What assumptions did you bring into your relationship with Jesus and how has He reshaped truth in your life through the journey?

2. How has brokenness or disappointment in life affected your relationship with God?

3. Have you ever known an extra measure of God's nearness when your spirit was poor or empty? How did it change you or sustain you?

4. As you take a quick spiritual inventory, are you living like a woman who has been given a spiritual inheritance? Are you operating in forgiveness, grace, mercy, etc?

5. Have you been waiting for healing or perfection before you could lay the offering of your life on the altar of God's love? What do you sense God is saying to you in this chapter about broken things and broken lives? Is He giving you a very specific action or attitude to try on?

2

WOUNDED

⁓

Blessed are those who mourn,
 for they will be comforted. (Matthew 5:4)

Mourning makes us poor; it powerfully reminds us of our small-
ness . . . [But] in our suffering, Jesus enters our sadness, takes us
by the hand, pulls us gently up to stand, and invites us to dance.
(Henri Nouwen)

I TOLD YOU THAT I AM DIVORCED.

A part of me wants to tell you all the details of each path I have
walked in this process, or at least as much as I can figure out. But
it will have to suffice for me to write very little. One of my godly
professors recently told me that what happens in private should be
spoken of in private. Private confession, private counsel, and private restoration. I believe his words have great value, and I intend
to adhere to their wisdom. But I will say that in the process of
divorce there was great pain, more than I could have ever imagined
and more than I will ever write about.

A couple of my closest friends have suffered through their
own version of different pain in recent years. And they have even
more friends who face multiplied heartaches. Several times I
have been cornered at church or in the grocery store by a person

who whispers. I am starting to realize that people who begin in whispers are hurting. I always know what's coming when they turn their eyes downward and begin to speak softly. *Can we have coffee? I don't think my marriage is going to make it. I just received some devastating test results. My husband lost his job. My son made a bad choice. Could I talk to you?*

I have decided that we are everywhere. There are so many of us. How did intense pain become epidemic? Why is so much suffering replicated in the homes and hearts of believers? I don't know how or why. Actually, at this point in my life, I know so much less than I thought I did before. I just know that life can hurt. It can hurt beyond words.

My close friends are just as stunned as I am at how life unfolds. When you get us all in the same room, we are one messy, worn-out bunch. It's like group therapy gone bad . . . godly people questioning what happened to our good effort, decent people wondering what in the world became of the neat little lives we were building. We are three people trying to pick up our million pieces, now scattered to the ends of the earth by the winds of agony and attacks that won't seem to retreat.

One night at dinner, I tagged us "the walking wounded," and it stuck. We decided there should be a club and parties for the other wounded, because no one should have to stand under this kind of pain alone. It's unbearable, truly unbearable, to suffer the burden of grief all by oneself. We also realized that others become the walking wounded for entirely different reasons than us, but the weight of their pain and mourning feels the same . . . a heaviness that is overwhelming . . . insufferable . . . suffocating.

I decided to write the charter for our club one afternoon just for fun. I know, I really do need a life, but what I realized was that it helped to put words to our pain. It went something like this:

The Walking Wounded Club Charter

We, the undersigned, have come to recognize that we belong to a distinct group of people, who shall hereafter be known as The Walking Wounded. We are the shell-shocked and hurting. We are the ambushed and abandoned. We are the dumbfounded and shaken.

Life, to us, feels like a dream gone haywire, someone else's nightmare. It has taken a while, but we have come to realize that we are not dreaming. These are not the lives we had planned, but we are fully awake and living nonetheless. We find ourselves walking in the direction of heaven, limping, bruised, battered, and weary, so very, very weary.

The Walking Wounded don't have many answers. Most of us aren't quite sure what just happened, how we got here, or where life is going. What did we do to cause all of this? What didn't we do? Good grief, it seems as though we were just muddling along and one day the world caved in on top of us.

The Walking Wounded are not proud. Many of us did nothing to deserve our heartache, but we're still embarrassed and ashamed. We have heard the rumors and screamed from the torture of their absurdity. We have lain in our beds, tightly wound into balls, just waiting and praying for the roof to fall in and take us right on up to heaven. And maybe more than anything, our swollen eyes have cried enough salty tears to empty the Pacific.

We are The Walking Wounded, truly. Some are bleeding profusely. Some have bandaged wounds that will need forever to heal. Some of us still need to be carried. We are doubled over in pain. Still seeing stars from the emotional right hook we never saw coming. Our bodies haven't yet caught up with our breath. We're afraid to stand up. Afraid to open our eyes and look out. Afraid that it's not over and more blows are coming. Afraid that we have deserved everything we got. Afraid to hope. Afraid to love. Afraid to believe. Afraid to touch. So very afraid that it could all happen again somehow.

We have decided to affiliate ourselves with one another for the purpose of companionship, strength, and shared burden. Some days there is relief in not having to explain the waves of depression, the struggle with bitterness, or the outbursts of anger. The members of The Walking Wounded understand. No one has to say anything. You see, The Walking Wounded will become the walking dead if they have no one to support them, no courage to press into, and no one to remind them of our Great Hope for the future.

Your registration for this club came as an invisible attachment. It may have been attached to a docket number, a CAT scan report, death certificate, pink slip, missing persons report, or any other life event that came like a deluge, a torrent of raging water that made you think you would surely drown.

There is no initiation required. As a matter of fact, you've had enough initiation already. You're in the club.

There are no dues or fees. One broken heart grants a lifetime membership to its owner.

Emergency meetings may be called by anyone at any time for any reason. There will also be parties—you heard us—parties for The Walking Wounded, to remind us of God's goodness and the life that awaits. And dancing, yes, there most certainly should be dancing with no one allowed to stand around wishing they could join in.

The Walking Wounded Club is chartered for the purpose of healing. We want to run toward it, get next to it, and stand underneath it. Both individually and corporately, we commit to pursue healing at any cost. It seems as if we have already lost everything, so what should it matter that we pay any price necessary for real healing of the soul. We will wait alongside one another for the healing only time can muster. We will hold one another until there is a light in the darkness. We will cry and pray and hold out hope, realizing that sometimes "there is no way to get through it, except to walk through it."

*And so, with this charter, we officially become The Walking Wounded.
Of course we already were and no one needed it to be official, but now we
have one another. Our grieving is shared. There is encouragement for the
soul. And shoulders to share the burden. And the prayers of fellow members.*

*And should one of us forget, let us all be quick to remind the fellow-
wounded that the God of heaven and earth holds us. He binds up the brokenhearted. He gives soul healing and unimaginable hope to every one of
us who will call on His name. His plan for each of us is still good. He is
still amazing. He is forever, and this season of mourning will one day pass
away because of His faithfulness and His love.*

There you have the charter. Maybe you already have a lifetime
membership. Maybe you have a friend who belongs. Maybe an
intense season of mourning qualifies you for VIP status. Either
way, when you are mourning or grieving or aching with sadness,
your heart has invisibly pledged to a kindred society called The
Walking Wounded.

The Waves of Mourning

I took my children to the beach this summer. The most fun thing
that we did, and the most stressful, was standing in the water,
which was up to my waist, jumping waves. After each wave crashed
around us, I would count, one, two, three, four. Hour after hour
that week, it felt as though all I did was count to four, looking for
my four familiar heads and giggles. I would stand in the water side-
ways with one eye on the coming waves and one eye on the children. At least two of them were attached to me most of the time.
Someone would yell, "Here it comes!" and we'd time our group
jump to keep our heads above the water.

But every once in a while, we'd have our backs to the ocean, talking, standing calmly in what seemed to be a respite from the pounding, and before anyone could shout, we'd be overtaken by a tsunami that came out of nowhere. We would be laughing and spitting out seawater, and I'd usually have to reach over and grab William by the arm to pull him out of the undertow. He's the kind of kid who always comes up smiling, wide-eyed, and begging for more. The rest of us weren't so excited about being lost under an ocean of water . . . it felt scary and the water tasted bad, and what used to be fun became the battle of our scrawny selves against the entire Atlantic Ocean. After a while, muscles begin to ache, the resolve to jump wanes, and the ocean always wins.

A few months ago it felt as though I was standing with my back to the ocean and a tidal wave of grief overtook me. I don't know were it came from, except somewhere out there in the sea of my pain and suffering. I thought I was standing in a respite, but before I knew it, I had gone under.

I have learned to realize that I've been pulled under when all I want to do is sleep. Eight or ten hours in a night won't be enough. Everything makes me sleepy. I can only do what is mandatory . . . get the children ready for school, make their breakfast, sign their papers, fake a smile, and crawl back to bed with my clothes on as soon as they are gone. Set my clock to get up and do car pool in the afternoon, stumble through dinner and baths and, finally, back to the comfort of my bed. All alone. Aching. Crying. Grieving my life. Sleepy.

One of my best friends is a stay-at-home mom with little kids who are friends with my kids. She also happens to be a family doctor who is practicing a few days a week at a local interfaith clinic.

"I might be depressed," I told her one afternoon at her house.

"You're entitled," she said. "Why don't you step into my office," she offered after we finished picking up cat costumes and plopped onto the couch. "Let's go through the symptoms of clinical depression and see where you are."

She carefully walked me through the questions she would ask any patient at the clinic. I answered honestly, hoping she'd find something going on with me that she could fix.

"You don't have a depression that I would want to treat with medicine," she said, "but you're grieving. The broken heart has to grieve."

"I thought I'd be stronger than this by now. The whole ebb-and-flow thing stinks. I don't like being pulled under by these waves. Some days I just want to give up and let it take me out to sea."

"How about just rolling over on your back and learning to float for a while? Remember that in order to float, you have to relax your body. And you have to breathe to float. When you are stronger you can turn yourself around and swim to shore, but it's not time yet. Sometimes you just have to keep breathing and grieve."

Sometimes indeed.

Sometimes life takes you under. The soul is raw. The pain returns in waves. And the walking wounded truly have to mourn.

So That You Can Be Comforted

Jesus said, "Blessed are those who mourn, for they will be comforted." Funny thing about grief and mourning: we want someone to take it away or something to numb it away, but no one or nothing can. The books say that it's healthy. Psychologists reason that it's necessary. I am learning that

> *I am learning that the only way to the other side is through.*

the only way to the other side is *through*. The difficulty is that we don't think we can get through because it's so incredibly lonely to grieve. Unfortunately there are no interstates through mourning. The only path is poorly marked, fraught with potholes, sharp turns, and steep, harrowing cliffs on either side. And it's always dark when we're grieving, a deep, dark night of the soul.

At the height of my pain, a friend knocked on the door with a loaf of bread. She said, "I don't know what to do, so I made you food." We laughed. I cried. She tried. Nothing helped. I don't even think I touched the bread, but I was grateful. Still lonely, but grateful that people wanted to take my sadness away.

In my sadness, I have felt so much like a baby girl. The girl that just wants someone to come and make it all better. The baby who cries until she's all cried out or until she's cried herself to sleep.

Have you ever seen a little baby pitch a fit? A full-blown, I'm-mad-and-sad-and-nobody-can-make-me-glad fit? Food won't work. Toys are thrown. Being held is awful. The crib is a jail. I'd watch one of my own toddlers act ridiculous and think, *They're just going to have to give it up.*

The grown-up soul becomes rightfully discontent in our grief. Nothing brings relief in our loss, and eventually we just have to give it up. Jesus knew that after we'd tried everything else, one day we'd give ourselves over to mourning, the emptiness of knowing that we cannot recover our lost lives or lost loves or lost dreams. He knew that ultimately we'd have to look straight into our agony and stop avoiding it. We'd have to hold up our sorrow, remember what was, accept what's gone, and cry until the ocean of our pain is empty.

Jesus told His followers on the hillside that when the tears are flowing and the pain is real and we have become the walking wounded who finally crawl into the presence of God, then we are blessed. Our lives can be a beautiful offering because the empty soul finds itself before the only One who can heal. We've tried every quick fix available. We've numbed ourselves with food, addictions, obsession, or sin, but nothing worked, and all that's left is to mourn what was and what never can be.

I think Jesus wanted us to know that the only comfort that speaks stillness to the squalling soul is supernatural. The things we try to do for ourselves can be distracting, but real comfort happens in the arms of God, the One who knows and understands and holds us in the pain. Jesus knew that He would become the sacrifice for our mourning, that He would become the Wounded Healer, the only hope the walking wounded will ever have.

> *When you are hurting, your head says that God is far away, but Jesus says, in fact, that God is closer than ever.*

When you are hurting, your head says that God is far away, but Jesus says, in fact, that God is closer than ever. This day if your soul aches and your heart mourns, please know that you are not alone—you're in the club and there are so many of us. But even more than the club, you are held and healed by the love of God. I think that Jesus wants you to know that

> *even when you are mourning, your life can still be a beautiful offering to God because in His presence and by His healing, your empty soul will find all the comfort it's aching for.*

The other day, one of the fellow-wounded was hurting. I dropped him a note via e-mail. I don't think he minds if I send it to you too:

My friend,

Remember the instruction about the long obedience? The call to keep being faithful no matter what. Just do that today. Lift up your head and turn in the direction of the Father. He'll take it from there. If He sends someone to carry you, then let them. If He calls you away for an hour, then go. If you can't find your next breath, then ask someone to give it to you.

He has you. I promise. I only know because I sat in the dark and waited for God. I doubted His return for me. I questioned His mercy. I grieved and still grieve the way life turns out. All I know is that He does come into our midnight. A faint glimmer at first, much slower than I had hoped . . . but He comes.

Jesus said that in our mourning, God is very close and we are blessed. Lean on the truth of His words. Believe what your head can't conceive. Trust through the darkest night.

Psalm 56:8 says that God keeps our tears in a bottle (NASB). I find great comfort in believing that He is close enough and cares enough to catch every one I have shed. Maybe from that container of His love, God tenderly refills the oceans of our souls after we've cried them dry.

Questions for Reflection and Discussion

1. Have you ever found yourself in a season of deep, dark mourning? How would you characterize your relationship with God during that time? Close or far away? Intimate or angry? Have you ever learned to grieve openly with God?

2. If you were to just "give it up" and trust God through a dark place or event, what would that look like? Is God asking you to trust Him where you cannot see? Is He asking you to wait for His promised deliverance? What steps can you take in your heart and life that would help you to wait for God to bring comfort into your darkness?

3. Remember that God's comfort is a blessing that He gives to you when you are mourning. Your responsibility is to offer your grief to God. How have you ever known His divine comfort in the past? Sometimes I have to "wait until God comes with His holy comfort." Are you willing to wait in the presence of God for an extra portion of His comfort? Does "waiting on God" mean that you give up other ways you may have tried to ease the pain?

4. Second Corinthians 1 says that one of the purposes of our suffering is so that "we can comfort those in any trouble with the comfort we ourselves have received

from God" (verse 4). Is God asking you to give away the comfort He has given to you? How? To whom? Where? I have found that giving myself away in the name of Jesus fills the empty places like nothing else can. Have you found that to be true for your life?

3

BEING YOURSELF

⌒

Blessed are the meek,
  for they will inherit the earth. (Matthew 5:5)

A devout life does bring wealth, but it's the rich simplicity of being
  yourself before God. (1 Timothy 6:6 The Message)

AS A FRESHMAN AT THE UNIVERSITY OF NORTH CAROLINA, I enrolled in the first semester of English just like everyone else. By the second week, we had an assignment. Write a paper about something lame. I can't remember. Maybe we had to write about the summer. Maybe it was dormitory etiquette. There was a paper about tying shoelaces, but that wasn't the topic for this composition. Whatever it was, I don't think I was particularly concerned about my ability to put it together. But lack of concern does have this way of coming back to get you. The day our teacher returned the papers dramatically affected my concern deficiency.

The grade for my first collegiate writing effort, the very first mark I received for anything post–high school, the evaluation assigned to my ponderings about something lame was a D+/F. I remember seeing stars, gasping for air, and wishing I were dead. It looked like I was going to flunk out of the big-shot university before I could even break in my new backpack. My poor parents. The embarrassment it would cause them. The money wasted. My roommate and I had bought matching comforters for our beds and everything. I wondered if I could get a refund on the two-semester, wishful-thinking meal ticket I had purchased.

So I did what any firstborn, pleaser, scared-to-death freshman does. I didn't tell a soul and made an appointment with my teacher. After I got to his office there was a lot of crying, all mine, of course, and after I'd wasted half a box of tissue, he said, "Angela, you got the highest grade in the class."

"Huh?"

"Yeah, of all the papers, yours was the best."

What kind of consolation was that? I was the lead sweat hog. The most prolific dud in the bunch. Either we were all losers or my show-off teaching assistant was trying to scare the spit out of thirty kids who were spending their parents' money. I'm still mad at him because it worked on both counts. That grade kept me petrified for the next four years, and his marks convinced me that I really can't write squat.

Just about every time I open my laptop, I remember that guy. And if I don't remember him, I think about the other great authors I've read, and I become afraid that I can't. It's easy to start believing that I can't write when I remember that I use way too many sentence fragments. Gobs of slang. And I'm not academic enough. I don't make detailed outlines. I just teach through Scripture with my stories.

I didn't know I was going to do this when I grew up, and neither did my guidance counselor, so we didn't plan effectively. I never had any training. I should have at least taken one creative writing class or journalism or something. People always ask if I was an English major. I spare them the first-paper story and say,

"No, a double major in economics and television production . . .
go figure."

Besides all that, I'm not a scholar. I want to be, though. Good
grief, I love the conversations, books, and debates. I read the nerdi-
est things and try my best to hang with heady theology. I love
being in the library with musty books and all those ideas to
absorb. I am such a bookworm, and I'm wild for the classroom
and syllabi-shock and taking notes so fast your head spins. But I
do know some scholars, and I also know better than to open my
mouth when I'm with them. I just listen, observe, learn. Don't say
anything. Besides, if I did have something pedantic to offer, it
would be filtered through this accent.

I guess I have an accent issue too. The issue is that I was raised
in the South and sound like it. I'm okay with that. The people who
live next door to me are okay with it too. We're kind of proud of
our unique intonation. We all understand each other just fine. But
I'm speaking in Detroit in a few months and already praying that
there won't be a language barrier. I have visions of people laughing politely, whispering to one another in confusion, then deciding,
"We can't understand a thing she's saying. Let's get out of here."

So there you have it, a nice sampling of my basic insecurities. I
become afraid that I can't write, I'm not a scholar, and the Southern
accent gives me away every time. Just a few of the reasons I think
God couldn't use a girl like me to write or speak.

A meek person is defined as one who is deficient in spirit or
courage, lowly, unassuming, without spunk or confidence. Jesus
seems to imply that the meek who are blessed have come to
accept their limitations, learning to be content before God with
how they have been put together. In the past, I have let my insecurities steal my courage and my vision. I would protest, "It's just
me," assuming that I could never be enough. Of course, God is

God and I never dreamed, not even for a second, what He had planned for me to do.

Sometimes, don't you just wonder what He was thinking? God knows it's just me, for goodness' sake. He knows I write like this, and He decided I should be born in the heart of the South where people grow up sounding like this. I imagine He listens to my protests and says, *I hear whining like this all the time. Why does everyone question My sovereignty? I am the Creator here, and I'm not surprised by the talent pool. I have always known it's just you, and I choose to use you anyway.*

I Need a Savior

I have been such a whiny-baby with God. His call on my life is to write and speak, giving out the truths of Scripture through sound teaching and stories. I have wanted to write all my life but didn't try until I was thirty-five because my stuff wasn't like anyone else's. I didn't know that could be a good thing. But I can become paralyzed, thinking I'm not as good as so-and-so. I don't teach like such-and-such. Maybe He should just send them instead. And while He's at it, He should probably send someone who sounds Midwestern.

Everywhere I go, I get a couple of sentences out and people cut me off with, "Where are you from?" Makes you a little gun-shy about what's coming next. I'm thinking either, *They like the accent, so turn it up* or *They hate the accent; quick, do your best Iowa imitation.*

I want to tell people about the love of Jesus so bad that I could burst, but I say to God, "It's okay if You pull the plug on this whole thing. There are speakers without accents. There are writers with perfect grammar. I'll understand."

I can too easily become discontent with my gifts. And when I do, I wander into fear. I want to be better than I am. I want to write and speak flawlessly before we put God's name to it. I want to honor God so much that I think it might be better sometimes if I just don't do anything. I don't want to be just me.

It's like the week before I began seminary, when I was sick, physically and emotionally sick. My friends were asking, "What in the world is wrong with you?" I was as stressed as anything, all self-imposed. I had already begun to imagine less-than-perfect results. I kept thinking, *How can you make less than an A in the Word of God? I mean, what would that reflect about your commitment level? How can you say, "I love You, God, but I only made a C in Bible"?* I was freaking myself out. Obviously, I knew very little about grace. The virus that caused my sickness was the weird notion that if I just tried hard enough then I could be the perfect Jesus girl.

But I can't. I have tried like crazy and I still can't.

One day I was beating myself up about something. Whining and wallowing in discontent magnified by doubt. My sister-in-law, Jodi, looked me square in the eye and said, "Angela, of course it's just you, and you will never be enough, you will never have all the answers, and you will never become the perfect Christian girl; that's why you have always needed a Savior. Not only does Jesus save you from your sin, He saves you from your weakness. He saves you from your flawed and fallen self. And He saves you from your doubts. He is enough every time you are not."

I think she set me free that day.

Hallelujah, I need a Savior! I NEED a Savior who is my Sustainer and Completer! It's okay not to be enough, because I was made to need the Son of God. I can't be sinless. I

> *It's okay not to be enough, because I was made to need the Son of God.*

need a Savior. I can't be flawless. I need a Savior. I can't be secure or confident without my Savior. I will never be the perfect speaker girl or amazing writer woman. I will never be enough all by myself, but I have a Savior and I can rest.

Have you ever been stopped dead in your tracks, thinking it's no use to try? Does an assumption like that keep you from dreaming? Did you believe the marks you made or the comments they gave? Has someone ever said, "You can't," and then you lived as if what was said was true? Does imperfection overshadow your giftedness?

If you have ever quit or thrown up your hands in frustration . . . If you've decided for sure that it's no use . . . If people said things that made you decide to stop living . . . If they stole your dreams and hauled off your courage and left you discontent and afraid . . . If you know it's just you and that this version of you will never be enough, then I have some good news today.

You need a Savior too.

Courage to Be Just Me

Yesterday we were at the neighborhood pool. I was overjoyed last week when I found an electrical outlet up there on the fence beside an umbrella. Now I can plug my computer in. This book might make its deadline. The kids are swimming to their hearts' delight while four lifeguards watch. And the pizza guy delivers any size you please, with a two-liter of soda, right to my new office. Please disregard any soggy Goldfish or Popsicle stains on the pages because I am also the keeper of snacks and goggles and sunscreen and hugs for when "Grayson was drowning me."

Anyway, yesterday a woman from Boston introduced herself to me and asked what I was working on. Right off the bat, I'm thinking, *She is not going to understand a word that I say, and she's going to hate what I do.* I am generally optimistic, but realism sometimes gets the best of me.

When I don't want someone to run away, I tell them, "It's a book for women about faith." When I want to scare them off, I say that I'm writing about Jesus. That one makes people at the pool need to find their children and people on airplanes need to take a nap. I told her the faith one, and we began a conversation that worked its way through the afternoon. After I'd walk around to check on the kids, she and I would chat for a few more minutes. We laughed about our accents and began to bond around the kiddie pool.

Eventually my family was hungry, and lucky for us, the pizza man was right on time with an extra-large cheese. My new friend and her children joined us. The kids swallowed theirs whole and were gone in a matter of minutes. I was tired of writing and made no effort to move. The woman from Boston wanted to ask questions.

"So you really believe this faith thing?"

Here we go, I thought, *this is where we will politely part company. I'm going to tell her the truth and see how long it takes for her to pack up her pool bag.* I said, "I do. I've decided to stake my whole life on it."

She didn't get that uneasy, I-have-to-find-the-nearest-exit look, and I was surprised. Matter of fact, she jumped right back in. "I go to church, but I'm scientific. I need more proof. Things in the Bible are confusing to me."

"Like what?"

"Like the walls of Jericho. I just can't figure out how they could fall down. Do you really believe they just came down after those people walked around them?"

"I do."

"I don't know; there's other stuff too. I've heard about the saved part, but I don't get the heaven thing. I'm a paramedic and I've helped a lot of people. That has to count for something when I get to heaven."

"The Bible says it counts for nothing if you don't know Jesus as your Savior."

"But I think that before you get to heaven, you have to learn how to forgive yourself."

"Jesus says that getting to heaven is about being forgiven by Him."

Our random conversation kept jumping around all over the place. Then I began to sense God's blessing. The pool fog was lifting, and I realized this woman's heart was engaged. God was doing something. I was there, and it seemed He wanted me to be a part of it. It felt as if the Holy Spirit was nudging, *Sit up here, Angela, and pay attention. We're getting ready to use you. Offer this woman the kingdom of God. Be meek. Be content with who you are in Christ, and tell her that stuff you're writing about. Tell her about the inheritance that can't be bought.*

Before I knew it, I was speaking with authority, just like I was best friends with God. I told her about my own doubts and my struggles with forgiveness. There were no language barriers because the Holy Spirit had introduced a woman from Boston to a woman in Knoxville. I wasn't a bit worried about choosing the right word or sounding scholarly. I didn't even remember to worry that she might not like what I said. It was just me, the girl who needed a Savior, telling someone else how to find Him.

Her questions took another path. "I've heard about the Tribulation, and I'm worried about that. I can't rest at night. It sounds awful. Everyone says the end is near. What if we have to go through that? Aren't you afraid?"

I knew that, truly, nothing inside of me was afraid. Quickly I thanked God for a soul peace I didn't even understand. I said to her, "I don't know what's going to happen. There are three different camps of thinking about when God is going to take us out of here.

But either way, I am okay. I know that I belong to God and that, in rapture or tribulation or death, I am His."

"How can you have that kind of faith?"

"It's a decision to believe that God is who He said He was, Jesus is His Son, and that His death paid for my sins. I have accepted by faith that it's all true. I've decided to put my burden down and rest in God as my Father and Jesus as my Savior."

"I think I have faith, but I can't lean into it."

"It seems like you don't have leaning faith because you aren't sure if you're saved."

"You're right, I'm not sure."

Wow. Right there in last year's one-piece, with greasy sunscreen hair, I could hear God using me to tell a woman about His love, strength, grace, and forgiveness. I didn't have to be the Bible Answer Woman. I didn't have to know even one Greek tense. I only had to be the woman God has shaped thus far. He could use me just like that.

I got to ask her my favorite thing in the whole wide world. "Would you like to be sure that you're saved?"

She said, "I would," and I told her.

"Sounds too easy." She made me grin.

"Why don't you think about it?" I offered.

She asked, "Can we talk about this some more on Monday?"

"Of course," I said. "I'd love to."

I floated home with the kids. Content that it was just me. I wish I was more sometimes, but I'm not, and yet I'm God-blessed anyway because I have a Savior.

Leaning into the Savior

Jesus' instructions to His followers in the When You Are's were so very insightful. He had to know that from their gratefulness and admiration, many would begin trying to outdo the others. Maybe they'd end up in the I-can-love-Jesus-more-than-you-can competition. He didn't want that craziness going on in His name. He'd had enough of the arrogant I'm-better-than-you Pharisees so He said to them, "I bless the meek."

You are blessed when you learn to be content with who you are and how I made you. Stop scrambling to look like the other guy. Quit imitating your neighbor and instead imitate Me. I put you together. The accent was on purpose. The introverted countenance was My idea. I realize your limitations. I am aware of your personality type. I am the designer. Just look at Me and rest in both your strength and your weakness. You are blessed when you can't be more, because I can. Turn in my direction. Be the woman I created. She is a beautiful offering.

I think Jesus was saying that when you are meek then you are well acquainted with your own flaws. The meek realize that they will never be enough and recognize that they will always need a Savior to complete them. Meekness is coming to see that you're not such a big deal after all and knowing when others might be more talented or poised. The meek are uncomfortable with their inadequacy because it's very humbling to realize that "it's just me." And yet that's the very place where Jesus can step in with His strength and give the blessing.

If we paraphrased this passage, maybe we could say,

When you are sure that you are not enough, in desperate need of the Savior's strength, then your life is a beautiful offering because God comes to the rescue with all the resources of His kingdom here on earth.

I am inclined to forget God's blessing for the ones who rest in their meekness. Sometimes I can work myself into a frenzy, making unfair comparisons about my work or my mothering or the scrapbooks I intend to begin for the children. Before I have to give a message, I'm usually in a room somewhere praying my guts out. That prayer almost always goes like this:

God, You know it's just me.
  I am fully devoted. I want all of me to belong to all of You. But if it's just me standing up there, we're in trouble. I need You to get there before me. I need You to push me aside. I need You to speak what I could never think. I will give out these words, but God, You have to show up with the power.
  Would You go before us in strength? Come with the might of Your Holy Spirit and do transforming life work that has nothing to do with me and everything to do with You. If You can use just me, then use me for Your glory. I am Your vessel. I want to love You with my life. I will do whatever You ask for Your sake and for Your renown.
  In Jesus' name, amen.

His Kingdom on Earth

Do you remember that the blessing for those who are poor in spirit is the kingdom of heaven? In that chapter, we talked about the inheritance, God's good gifts—that include mercy, power, forgiveness and more—that have been set aside for us because we now belong to Him. In this passage, Jesus says that the blessing for the meek, or those who recognize that "it's just me," is that they will partake of that same inheritance on earth. We don't have to wait for heaven to receive the inheritance—we can know the blessing of God's gifts for this earthly journey.

  Inheriting the earth is God's gift to the content. Everything that belongs to the Father belongs to you. Every need will be met.

Everything required will be provided. No need to jump up and down for attention. You don't have to cut in line to get ahead. You don't even have to cheat or worry or try to make yourself look better than you are.

God sees that it's just you. And He loves it when you lean into Him with everything you have and everything you don't have and trust. That's the kind of heart He's happy to bless. God comes to us when we're meek, when we're absolutely sure that we are a little fish in a big pond, and provides all that we need on this earth.

> When it is settled in your heart that you will never be enough, then the glory of God comes into focus.

Do you long to hear the compassionate grace of God today? Do you need a break from trying so hard and always coming up short? Would it soothe your soul to quit whining about your weakness and shout, "I need a Savior!"? 'Cause when you get it, when it is settled in your heart that you will never be enough, then the glory of God comes into focus. You see Him. Maybe for the first time, you see His splendor in light of who you are.

I wonder if God smiled while I cried that day in college. I wonder if He whispered, *Hush those little freshman fears. I am God. I make walls around a city fall down with a shout. I take girls who think they are flunking out of life and turn them into writers. I provide the bounty of the earth for those who know their own weakness. Do not fret. Do not be afraid. Look into My eyes and hear Me.*

I sent my Son because I know it's just you.

Questions for Reflection and Discussion

1. I'm sure that, just like me, you have plenty of reasons for believing God could never use a woman like you. When you think of your insecurities or flaws, what traits come to mind first?

2. Do you realize that God is not surprised by your insecurities and He wants to use you for His purposes anyway? Is there an area where God has been calling, but you have been dragging your feet, protesting that you're not enough yet?

3. You know that you need a Savior to be rescued from the penalty of your sin. How do you continue to need a Savior in your day-to-day life?

4. Would you say that you have learned to "lean into the Savior" with your life, or have you stiff-armed God, keeping your distance, never fully putting your weight down onto His promises?

5. God wants to show up in your life with the gifts of His kingdom when you have become content in your meekness. If you could choose three of God's gifts, which ones would you choose for your life and why? Did you know that it's okay to ask God to bless your life? It's okay to ask for the resources that only He can give.

4

FALLING IN LOVE

⌒

Blessed are those who hunger and thirst for righteousness,
*   for they will be filled. (Matthew 5:6)*

Like newborn babies, crave pure spiritual milk, so that by it you
may grow up in your salvation. (1 Peter 2:2)

I HAVE A FRIEND WHO'S IN LOVE.

Kind of.

It's only been a few dates, but she is swooning. Well, maybe just one date because I think she counts phone calls too.

We have a great time talking about her new love life because she's milking the silliness to the hilt. I laugh until I cry with her. The whole thing is a riot because she's forty-four years old, brilliant, typically steady and not given to so much drama. One time this guy called when I was with her. She looked at the incoming number on her cell phone and morphed into a fifteen-year-old before my eyes. Happy, tippy-toe dancing around the room before she answered it, just like one of those football players who ran the whole field for a touchdown. Howling with delight. High fives. What a show. What a nut. Then somehow she managed to pull herself back together long enough to say, "Hello," as if she had no idea who it was.

She says that when he calls, it makes her stomach hurt and she can't think of anything coherent to say. She says that he makes her laugh and no one has ever made her laugh before. She says that when he kissed her, she just about died and heard angels. She says that remembering their first dance takes her breath away, and that makes her stomach hurt all over again.

What a lovesick goofball.

He lives far away, so I asked if she thinks of him often.

"Think of him?" she screamed. "I can't get rid of him. I hear his voice in my thoughts and replay his tender words to me. I close my eyes tight and beg my head to remember what he looks like. I love to see his name in my e-mail in-box. I long to know him fully. Does he like jazz or Americana or neither? Does he prefer milk chocolate or dark? What makes him afraid? What gives him rest? I just know enough of him to make me want to know more."

That gaga friend of mine makes me smile. Every time I look at her she's grinning. I've never seen her act so ridiculous. Then again, I can't remember her more happy either. A smidgen of delight. The longing for more. Life and distance and a stomachache. The wait for the one you've always dreamed of. Anticipation. Hope for an empty heart. The rhapsody of falling in love.

My girlfriend hasn't known healthy, romantic love in more than twenty-two years. She has a lot of friends, beautiful children, and a great family. She is supported and cared for. But she is just like the rest of us . . . she was made for more. She was made for intimacy and passion. She was designed to long for romance. She eagerly desires the filling one man's attention seems to give. She is thrilled and silly and happy because God made this kind of falling so wonderful.

When I listen to her voice, watch the sparkle in her eyes, and bask in her lighthearted countenance, I wonder, *Why can't we all just keep falling in love?*

I have friends who've been married fifty-two years. They raised five children together and lost another to death. They live in a retirement village with other folks their age and do everything together. It's all these years later and they are still best friends.

He chauffeurs her to the mall and waits patiently for her to try on shoes or find a new lipstick. She wipes his chin when mayonnaise drips from his sandwich and makes sure his shirts are pressed just the way he likes them. They send each other cards. Leave each other notes. And hold hands like they just met. She still laughs at his old jokes, and he still calls her *Baby*. I watch them lean into each other affectionately and admire their mutual desire for one another.

One day I asked her, "How did you keep your relationship strong?"

She said, "We just kept falling in love."

⌒

Do you remember when you fell in love with Jesus? I do. It was the beginning of my sophomore year in college, and a girl on my hall invited me to a Fellowship of Christian Athletes meeting. A few hundred coeds my age were carrying Bibles into a room, and I'd never seen anything like it. We sang songs and someone told about a Jesus who meets you where you are, and then we held hands and prayed. For the first time in all my churchgoing days, I truly met Jesus there. I had heard of Him. His reputation was familiar to me. But over the next few weeks, I was introduced to the only One who has ever been able to fill the deepest yearning in my soul.

I spent the next years completely smitten. Everything finally made sense to me, and I was a fireball. I recall the passion of that time with great tenderness. I was so disciplined about my quiet times and ached with regret if I missed a day with God. Thoughts of my love for Him were woven into every part of the day. *How can I serve? Who can I tell? Where should I go in His name?* I truly hungered for His presence. My thirst could not be quenched. My soul had been empty and longed to be filled with His love. I wanted to spend the rest of my life falling in love with Jesus.

Hunger and Thirst

Jesus said that when you are hungry and thirsty for His righteousness, then you are blessed. It is beautiful to Him when we desire His presence and long for right living. Right living means that we begin to desire what God desires. It means that our longings begin to line up with His purposes and His plans. Our decisions get filtered through the grid of His instruction, our love begins to mirror the reflection of His love for us, and our motives are refined as we consider His will.

I think that the emotion of falling in love is a great picture of what Jesus meant. When you are in love there is an intense hunger and thirst, a passion for the one you love that can parallel our spiritual craving for God and His righteousness. We can fall in love with Jesus and yet, spiritually, there will have to be an ongoing choosing to keep falling in love.

My friend is falling in love because of her desire and because she has met a man who is gentle and honorable. Her empty heart yearns to be filled. She's just a girl who was made to fall for the guy. The heart's craving to give and receive love is profound and intense.

My older friends kept falling in love for fifty-two years, and the result is an incredibly beautiful friendship and marriage. They told me there were seasons when passion waned. To counter the hollowness in those times, each one chose to do whatever was necessary to fall in love again, more deeply than before. Their continued falling is the product of choosing, over and over, to return to love.

Most people cannot sustain the intensity of "falling in love" with someone for a lifetime, but they can choose to return to the memory and the power of when they first met for healing, renewal, and focus. In our spiritual lives, much the same thing can happen. Life can be distracting and our hearts can wander away from our first love with God. Our hunger and thirst can wane.

I have not been able to sustain a consistent, fervent passion with God all by myself. When my whole life fell apart and every prop went away, I found myself as empty of passion as I have ever been. I wasn't hungry or thirsty for righteousness in those months, and I certainly wasn't falling in love with God. I was alone and afraid that I had been abandoned. I was desperate for answers that only time could bring. We can all become spiritually dry for so many different reasons.

But God has an incredible love for us, and He never turns away, even from our emptiness. He never stops pursuing His beloved. He never withdraws His affection. He never quits choosing to love you and me.

The blessing of being spiritually filled is attached to being hungry for God. Sometimes we can fall into a sentimental routine. We can go through the motions without a trace of desperate longing. In the routine or even in our spiritual slumber, we are still held by God, yet living outside this blessing of filling. Most of the Christian women I talk to speak to me about their emptiness. We will remain empty apart from a desperate desire.

I am coming to know a sweet soul healing because I finally asked God to do what I could not do for myself. I asked Him to make me hungry and thirsty again. I imagine that there might be people who have known a lifetime of consistent spiritual passion, but over the years, my consistency has been interrupted by babies, fatigue, disappointment, and even now, the overwhelming schedule of our lives. But the more I know what His filling is like, the more I am deciding to ask God every day to make me hungry. I desire the blessing of being filled by His presence. Even in my inconsistency, I am choosing to pray for more and more of this When You Are.

Our passion can be inconsistent, but when it is present—when you are falling in love with God just as you are hungry and thirsty for Him, then you are blessed. Does your heart cry out for this blessing? Do you long to know again His tender filling for your soul? Then maybe we could say,

> *Life is a beautiful offering when you are crying out for God to come and make you hungry for His righteousness, because He is the only One who will satisfy your spiritual appetite with the food that can fill your soul.*

Jesus said the passion that pleases Him is like hunger and thirst—consuming desire that cannot be stilled until our spiritual needs have been met in the pursuit of knowing Him more.

I imagine that most of Jesus' listeners that day were thirsty and hungry. Thirsty for healing and freedom. Hungry for deliverance and blessing. Maybe they were just beginning to realize that they were listening to the only One who could quench their thirst and feed their hunger.

Jesus said to them, *This is good. I bless your hunger and your thirst. It's beautiful when you surrender to your spiritual appetite and do what-ever it takes to feed your soul with My goodness, My virtue, and My example. I love it when you run after My right living like you cannot sur-vive without it.*

The Order of His Blessings

It's interesting that Jesus placed this instruction to hunger and thirst after righteousness in the When You Are's. It's gracious of Him. And so very understanding. Look at the positioning of His words. He could have brought up this righteousness thing right off the bat, but He didn't. First, He said that your life is beautiful to Him when you are poor in spirit, when you are mourning, and in your meekness, when you have learned to be content with who you are. He began this powerful sermon with incredible blessings of grace and mercy for His followers. Now, after we've begun to hear His heart of compassion in the first three When You Are's, Jesus changes gears a bit and tells us that when we desire His righteousness, our lives are also blessed.

I want to pursue righteousness every single minute, with every breath I have. That is my desire. But in the context of this sermon, it sounds as though Jesus already knew it probably wouldn't happen that way. He knows it's just me and He knows it's just you. He spoke into our weakness first, and then He called us toward a diligent pursuit of His teachings. He let us know that He is aware of our fragile condition . . . the weakness of our flesh, best intentions that fail, and the way the world can take you by surprise.

We're going to hear it over and over in this sermon: Jesus guides us toward Christlikeness and yet remembers the fallenness of our humanity. He wants us to long for right living just as we desire human love or food. He wants us to come into His presence with that kind of

Jesus guides us toward Christlikeness and yet remembers the fallenness of our humanity.

intensity, but the order here: poor in spirit, mourning, meek, is intentional. He meant to give the other blessings first. Not because one is more important than the other, but because we needed to hear His call to righteousness couched inside the truth of His compassion.

This teaching about hunger and thirst is resting in the teaching about being poor in spirit and mourning. Can you hear the heart of the Father in this? Jesus says that our God understands. We are blessed when we pursue righteousness, but He told us first that even in our lack or difficulty or imperfection, we can still be a beautiful offering. I want to be strong and focused and disciplined in my pursuit of Christ. But sometimes I have been poor or wounded and without an appetite for the things of God.

These are the When You Are's, and I am so grateful for that. The primary call of the disciple is to love God with heart, soul, and mind, but I don't always get there. I fell head over heels in love with Christ, but my passion is not without flaw. Sometimes the fireball has only been a flicker.

Listen to the order of His heart.

> When you are poor in spirit,
> When you are mourning,
> When you are meek,
> When you are hungry and thirsty for righteousness . . .

Can you hear the compassionate heart of Christ saying, *I love it when you return. When your appetite is renewed. When you fall in love again. When you want Me more than anything on this earth?*

When you and I are starving for God, He calls it beautiful and blessed.

More Deeply

Maybe you haven't been hungry for a God-life in a while. Maybe you have wanted to be passionate for God, but there were things to do and the time just got away from you. Maybe you have heard your spiritual stomach growl but tried to ignore the rumbling. Wherever you are in your life with God, no matter what you have been doing until now, I want you to hear Jesus say, *Blessing awaits those who hunger for My righteousness.*

To be hungry means to eagerly desire or to crave because of emptiness or a weakened condition. We are all fairly familiar with our weak and empty places. We spiritually trip over that stuff all the time. Most people know they're needy, they just don't realize the soul is craving God.

> When you and I are starving for God, He calls it beautiful and blessed.

The other day, Taylor and I hung out with some middle schoolers. There was one kid who was miserable all day long. I called him "Sunshine." He never smiled. Nothing was funny to him. He was too cool for the whole wide world. He'd move from thing to thing, but nothing made him happy. Taylor and I were talking about it later. That kid was so lost. So empty. So obviously in pain. What could we do? We discussed recommending a counselor or new activities for his boring life or a family meeting with his parents. Taylor finally said, "Mom, the bottom line is, this kid needs Jesus." The bottom line indeed. That empty kid needed to fall in love with the only Person who could fill his soul.

Do you feel empty or numb to life and your circumstances? Would you say that you feel lost or abandoned or afraid? Have you been spiritually sleeping for more years than you can remember? Does your life obviously lack the power of the presence of God? Maybe you realize that you have never fallen in love with Jesus. Or maybe it's been a very long time and you have forgotten about a passionate life with Him. Either way, the blessing of being filled by the God of heaven is waiting for you.

What if we just went for it and decided to fall in love with Jesus more deeply than we have ever known? What would that look like? What would it feel like? You may not be perfect in your desire, but when you are hungry for God, He moves in with the filling of His blessing.

I think about my girlfriend. She models for us the beautiful emotion of falling in love. Maybe to hunger and thirst for the righteousness of Christ would look a lot like her surrendered heart:

- Jesus would always be in your thoughts and you'd be planning when you could see Him again. You would think about when you could be alone with Him, just to hear His voice or share your heart or sit quietly in His presence.

- You'd want to weave His person into every area of your life. You'd begin to reorder your commitments around Him. You'd change the way you do things so that He could be included.

- In this hunger for relationship, you'd want to be restored to Jesus quickly. You'd ask for forgiveness as soon as you realized your shortcomings. You'd work through mistakes, misunderstandings, and failures until they're resolved so that your bond remained intact.

- You'd plan your future differently because you would be pursuing Jesus. You'd be free to dream more courageous dreams with His love and His filling in your life.

Every time I meet someone who has just fallen in love with God, I'm a little jealous. They're so giddy and alive. They are hungry and thirsty for the person of Christ. They've invited half the neighborhood over to watch the *Jesus* film. They're giving out the forgiveness they just received all over the place. Addictions are beginning to lose their hold. Wounds are being healed. The old is passing away and everything is becoming new. They make me want to know God more deeply. Their infectious joy inspires me to crave His passion. I want to fall in love again.

Maybe it's really possible to keep falling in love. Maybe the Creator wants to keep bringing us back to life, afresh and anew. Could it be that our big God can give us a desire for right living beyond anything we have ever known? Perhaps we have forgotten who God is?

I can get so caught up in my Day-Timer that I forget what's going on in heaven. God is on the throne of all creation where He reigns in splendor. Angels are before Him and around Him and below Him, singing praises. The Holy Spirit is interceding for my life and yours day and night. Jesus sits at the right hand of the Father, preparing an eternity for you and for me. And the eyes of God search the earth for those who would humble themselves, fall upon His mercy, and beg Him to make them thirsty again.

Our God is able, so very able, to fill you and me with renewed passion for righteousness. He is more than ready to make us hungry. He can't wait to watch us fall in love again.

⌒

Maybe you recall a time when you were excited about Jesus. Maybe you remember it as a phase, a part of your childhood, or as a dramatic life experience somewhere along the way. Would you like to yearn for a God-life again? Do you want to keep falling in love? Do you wait like a prisoner to be freed from the chains of guilt and sin? Has it been so very long since you were hungry or thirsty for righteousness?

Then sink to your knees and pray. Lie on your face if you can. The One who fills has been waiting for your turn in His direction. Jesus still meets you where you are. In your turning and praying, God promises His blessing. He will not be put off if you come to Him in truth and pray something like this,

Lord, I am not hungry or thirsty for righteousness. I have become numb to longing for You. I can't remember what it was like to be in love, and I'm not sure I can even return. My heart is tired. My soul is empty. I have tried on my own and failed. My only option is for You to do something. Would You make me thirsty? Would You make me hungry? Would You make me want You more than anything?

Sometimes in my life, God has answered prayers instantly. But prayers like these usually require a commitment on my part. A commitment to continue coming into His presence. Seeking His power. Bombarding heaven with desperate prayers for strength. God will do the work that you can't. He will restore what has been lost and renew what you thought was dead. So keep praying until He makes you hungry and thirsty. Persist in prayer until you know that you're falling in love again.

Do you realize what the blessing of your hunger will be? A life free of guilt and sin. A life devoted to the teachings of Christ. A life that reflects the grace and mercy of a loving God.

They say that when you fall in love, the two of you begin to look alike. May it be so. Oh, sweet Jesus, may it be.

Questions for Reflection and Discussion

1. Recall the time you fell in love with Jesus.

2. Do you hunger and thirst after Jesus with the same intensity still? Why or why not?

3. Do you understand from the order of His blessings that God is not expecting "flawless righteousness"? He realizes the limitations of your humanity. He knows it's just you and me. Can you come to Jesus with the truth of wherever you are and humbly ask Him for greater hunger and thirst?

4. What if Jesus rekindled and flamed the fire of your passion for Him? How would that change your life?

5. A woman who is being filled with the righteousness of God is amazing. She has a God-given confidence that is captivating. Is there a thing or a person that you have expected to be your filling apart from God? Is there a dependency that needs to be given up so that you may be filled by the only One who can give you strength?

5

A FRIEND OF SINNERS

~

Blessed are the merciful,
for they will be shown mercy. (Matthew 5:7)

Who is a God like you? . . . You . . . delight to show mercy.
(Micah 7:18)

ON OUR SUMMER VACATION, WE DIDN'T GET TO CHOOSE who sat beside our beach umbrella.

For most of the week it was three grandparents with a two-year-old girl. She was cute, but I guess they affectionately called her name six hundred times in four days, so the cute factor began to fade. I don't think any of us will soon forget adorable little Lexi, who had three grown-ups wrapped around her tiny pinky. To say they were taken with her would be mild. They were crazy in love. I brought my four kids out for the day, each with towel in hand and carrying some water. Lexi had enough toys, snacks, and entertainment to run an amusement park. But the adoring ones were happy to do it.

Never mind that the grandparents began drinking beer around 10:00 A.M. and kept it coming as freely as waves pounding the shore. They also talked loud and chain-smoked, and it was a big, hairy deal every time one of them needed to hide from the wind to relight. This was evidently their lifestyle, because at seventy years old, no one seemed affected by the beer, and the baby sat in their laps eating fruit snacks as if it was normal to breathe smoky air. All in all, they were a pretty cordial bunch under the umbrella beside us. My kids were grossed out, but we were polite after I rebuked them for gagging loudly about the smoke. "Breathe somewhere else," I told them.

Then Friday came. It was the Fourth of July. By midafternoon a friend of a friend showed up to hang out with the grandparents. His name was Mike, and he was twenty-nine. He came down into the sand pulling a cooler on wheels with a backpack chair hanging from his shoulders. He hollered, "The party is here!" and they shrieked with joy. Hugs. Kisses. Obvious delight over Mike and his rolling party.

I'm so glad the children were in the water when Mike showed up because they missed the traveling salesman show where he displayed his wares. First he popped open the backpack chair and positioned it for maximum sun exposure. From its pocket, he pulled out sunscreen, a deluxe sound system, a CD collection complete with jazz, Sinatra, and Elvis, castanets for shaking in rhythm to the music (I'm not making this up), and pornographic magazines that he shared with the giddy grandparents and then, thankfully, put away.

Next was the cooler. There were large, hand-painted glasses that he showed all around, a bag of ice, four different flavors of vodka, and a variety of juices depending on his fancy. With my neighbors' umbrella only a few feet away, I stared straight out at my children in the ocean, but couldn't help getting the lowdown on his week at work, his thoughts about casual sex, his penchant for 900 numbers, and dancing in the sand. It was as if one person showed up and took up the whole beach. There was no avoiding it; Party Mike had come to play and moved in right beside me.

Now there I was, a forty-year-old God-fearing mother with four kids at a family beach, momentarily dazed by the vast array of everything I have tried to protect my children from. For at least the first twenty years of my life with Christ I was a five-star legalist. On the beach that day, I felt it all beginning to come back to me with a fury: *Get out of here, Angela, run away from this mess. What a sad guy. What a sick bunch of people. Losers. Sex addicts. Alcoholics. Heathens . . . Sinners.*

Somewhere in my haughty judgment the word *sinners* came to mind. When I heard myself call them sinners, I decided to stay put. Because right after I labeled them *sinners* in my head, my heart reminded me that Jesus was *a friend to sinners,* and I am a sinner and He has been my friend.

A little vodka later, the grandparents took the baby up to the room, and Mike introduced himself and began talking toward our umbrella as though we were at his party. "How many kids you got?" he asked.

"I have four and their four cousins came with us, so that's eight."

"You know, I could help you keep an eye on them, 'cause that's the kind of man I am."

"Great. I'll point them out and you just tell me if you see anyone misbehaving."

He looked patiently at everyone I pointed to. But the sun and the vodka must have been working in tandem because he said he needed to sit down. Eight was more than he could handle at the moment.

Then he said, "I'll tell you the best way to raise them kids."

"Sure, I'd love to hear."

"When they're about fifteen, you start getting them their own room at the beach, let 'em smoke and drink and watch anything they want all night. Just make sure they're safe. And make sure you talk to them about it. Open communication, that's the key."

"Really? That's what you think I should do?"

"Yep, look at me. I was raised like that and I'm okay. Been partying since I was in junior high, and I'm good."

"You know, Mike, you could be right. That may be the way to raise children. But you could be wrong. I've decided to take another path with the kids. We have boundaries for their physical and spiritual safety. I pray over them every day and ask God to guard their hearts and minds."

"Hmmm. Guess that's one way to do it," he said. "It sounds a little tight, but you seem pretty cool."

If you only knew how uptight and not-cool I have been, I thought.

"You like this music?" he asked, bobbing his head to a light jazz instrumental.

"Actually, I like it very much," I replied.

About that time, one of the children walked up and I could see the freak-out look in his eyes, *Mom is in her bathing suit talking to a man with a cigarette in one hand and a big glass of whatever in the other.*

"Honey, I want you to meet Mike," I said.

"Hey," he mumbled.

"Dude." Mike nodded his head and replied.

I went over to our chair to get whatever my child needed, and I could feel the legalist-in-training staring at me. I decided it was time for some retraining. "You know, sometimes God puts people beside your umbrella that you wouldn't have chosen. Don't you think it's cool of Him to introduce us to a guy who doesn't act like us, so we can be nice to him and tell him about Jesus?"

"I guess so," he said, with a hint of doubt in his voice, and ran off.

I turned back toward Mike, deciding it was time to get down to the faith talk. He was over in his chair, with his music and his glass of vodka . . . passed out. *Dang it*, I thought, *I was just getting ready to tell him the stuff that could change his life.* I kind of shuffled back to my chair, frustrated with myself and disappointed. I sat there counting eight children and wondering why God put a big ole sinner right beside me if he wasn't going to stay awake long enough for me to share the gospel.

As clear as anything, I heard in my spirit, *I put him beside you to see if you'd be his friend.*

Oh.

The Voice of Mercy

God knows me pretty well by now. He knows that I have not always befriended fellow sinners. He knows that I have moved away, kept my distance, and felt afraid. How did I become so judgmental and awful? How could I have come to believe, somewhere in my subconscious, that just talking to someone who is lost in sin would displease God? I think I had taken verses like these,

> Do not be yoked together with unbelievers. For what do righteousness and wickedness have in common? Or what fellowship can light have with darkness? . . . What does a believer have in common with an unbeliever? . . . "Therefore come out from them and be separate." (2 Corinthians 6:14–17)

> Do not love the world or anything in the world. If anyone loves the world, the love of the Father is not in him. (1 John 2:15)

and made ridiculous rules out of them.

Scripture teaches us not to become partners or companions of unbelievers, fools, and the blatantly sinful. Don't marry them. Don't go into business with them. Don't become social companions. Don't tie yourself to these folks. Jesus never said not to speak to them. Matter of fact, He modeled incredible care and mercy for sinners. He broke tradition and rules and spoke to them, ate with them, and gave compassion to them. He demonstrated physical, spiritual, and emotional mercy. And He made it freely available to everyone. He made it freely available to me.

In this last season, life has pounded on my door with a fury. I have been in ministry for almost twenty years. Sometimes on staff at a church, sometimes teaching a women's bible study, sometimes writing, and sometimes on the road. In between and through all the events of my life, there has been an unparalleled knowing that I am supposed to study and give out the truth of God's Word. Then I was divorced.

Remember that I have been a legalist. We are the ones who throw stones. We are quick to judge without knowledge. We feed rumors and incline our heads to hear more. We label the messy people and gossip about the sinners and shake our heads in disgust. And when you have been a legalist in ministry, it's not pretty. And it's not ministry. And it couldn't possibly be what Jesus had in mind when He said, "Go and teach them about Me."

So in divorce, I expected God to put a *D* on my back and send me to the end of the line. I was sure that He would say, "I can't use you anymore. Your days in front of people in My name are over. You will still make heaven, but maybe you should run along to law school and find something else to do with your life." I guess I expected God to label me the way I had labeled others.

I called everyone I had been associated with and told them what was happening. It was as painful a truth as I have ever spoken. The shame was huge. I laid everything about ministry down and fully expected that it would go away forever. And then I wound myself tightly into a ball and waited for the judgment that was sure to come. And some came, randomly, from the weirdest places and people. But more than anything, I began to hear the voice of Mercy call my name. And then one day, Mercy said, "Stand up. I have work for you."

"But there's a *D* on my back and my life is broken," I protested.

"The *D* must be covered by the blood of Jesus, because I can't see it," Mercy replied.

I had forgotten that in my deepest pain, I had begun to pray, *God, please have mercy on me. Send mercy, O Father, send mercy.*

And He did.

⌒

When our God who is Mercy comes like a shout into your darkness, when the Father stoops down and tenderly picks up the pieces of your broken life, when Jesus steps in front of what you could have deserved, and when the Lord of heaven says, "I still want you," after you thought no one would, it is the most amazing truth of all. I have been overwhelmed by this lavish kingdom gift called mercy.

Can you imagine the hearers of Jesus' sermon? All they had ever known were rules. Can you envision the lives they were leading and the attitudes they held? I can. Jesus stood up that day and took aim at the legalists by teaching,

When you are merciful to others, then you shall receive mercy for your own soul.

Can you hear Him saying,

It is a beautiful offering to Me when you lay down your judgment and choose compassion. When you love others the way I love you, when you hold back the consequences they could have deserved, and when you treat them the way you'd like to be treated, then you shall receive mercy as well.

Meeting Mercy

In God's economy, you get what you give. And Jesus taught that when you give mercy, it's given back to you.

I have a friend who needs mercy. She is a believer. She is on several committees at her church. She has children and a loving husband. And about five years ago, she began drinking in secret. It was a way to numb the pain and heartache and disappointment. In the beginning she drank only every few months, but now she wants to drink every day. Her husband knows and a few friends know and now a counselor knows. The counselor said that she needs to attend Alcoholics Anonymous meetings. She needs to be with others who battle the same struggle. But she is fighting against going with everything she has.

Yesterday she said that "godly people don't have these struggles. What would people at church say if they knew? I am a complete failure. I am so ashamed. I can't go to one of those meetings. I'm not like those people. My problem's not that big."

I have promised to drive her to a meeting and push her in the door. She can listen to me talk about mercy, read about it, even sing about it, but nothing will impact her soul until she hears Mercy call her name. I think she'll meet Mercy face-to-face at the very first AA meeting I can get her to. I believe she'll finally feel what grace feels like. I think she will be relieved to find there are people who can relate to her struggles without judgment. I can't wait until she meets Mercy, so I call her every day to tell her she is loved, that God is big, and we've got a meeting to get to.

How about you? Sometimes you have to meet Mercy for the first time so that you can learn to give mercy. Have you ever known what it feels like to be spared from consequences, forgiven of your sin, or rescued from the pit of despair? Jesus says, *Turn in My direction, move toward My voice, let Me show you the mercy.*

Because when you have been shown mercy by your Father in heaven, you cannot keep it in inside. People who have been given mercy want to hand it out freely and generously. Once you have known the indescribable joy of receiving love when you had expected judgment, there is no containing the lengths you will go to to give it away.

And so the life inclined toward mercy becomes a beautiful offering to God. In your great need, you can turn your aching heart toward the Father and ask for His mercy.

> *People who have been given mercy want to hand it out freely and generously.*

From the riches of His lavish love, He will tenderly give all that you need. Humbled by such a gracious gift, your heart will long to share with others who need mercy too. And when the one who gives mercy remains in the presence of God, all the mercy required is continually being provided.

Inclined Toward Mercy

You see, we don't get to choose who sits beside our beach umbrella. Nor do we select the person in the cubicle beside us, the uncle we've become related to by marriage, or the neighbor who just moved in next door. We can't control the choices of wayward children or wayward parents or wayward friends.

The gift that God calls pleasing is your mercy toward the ones you haven't chosen and the ones who make decisions you'd never choose. They can be fallen, struggling, disappointing, or downright embarrassing. Maybe they are people you love or a stranger who rear-ended you in the parking lot. However people come into your life, I can assure you that they are seen and known by God.

He calls it beautiful when you give to anyone the mercy He has so freely extended to you.

When your soul is being perfected by the presence of Mercy, then judgment begins to fade, the made-up rules don't matter so much anymore, and what everyone might think becomes ridiculous. The heart gets tender toward people in sin, the snare of their addictions, the depth of their pain and unspoken suffering.

Life gets messy when you begin to give out mercy, but when you're giving out mercy, you don't care about the mess anymore. Some people won't understand. They didn't understand Jesus either. Some will judge. Bank on it, someone will doubt your motives or your heart or your radical choice to extend mercy. Give on, because blessed are the merciful. I expect that no matter how much you give, you will always receive more than you have given. God's accounting is amazing.

Life gets messy when you begin to give out mercy.

One warning: This blessing probably won't work if you want to hold on to your legalism or if you value rules more than souls. Mercy might make you uncomfortable and blow away the box you've drawn around God. If you begin to give out mercy, things are going to change. You are going to begin to look into the eyes of people and hurt for their pain. You are going to hear yourself offer light into their darkness. You will start to love the unlovely.

Who knows, one day you might just become a mercy fanatic. You could begin to reflect the heart of Jesus to everyone you meet. And you'd watch people huddle in the corner and speak in judgmental whispers about you, "Look at her over there . . . she's a friend to sinners."

Questions for Reflection and Discussion

1. Has legalism, judgment, or rule-keeping ever kept you from hearing the voice of Mercy? How?

2. How has God come to you as Mercy? How has He surprised you with grace and tenderness?

3. Why is it sometimes easier to choose judgment over compassion and mercy?

4. If a beautiful life means extending mercy where you have chosen condemnation in the past, what does that mean for the people you are closest to? Is there someone you love who needs to receive your mercy?

5. If the blessing of giving mercy is receiving mercy, then what are the obvious implications of becoming a woman of mercy? Becoming a woman who is a friend to sinners?

6

PURE IN HEART

~

Blessed are the pure in heart,
  for they will see God. (Matthew 5:8)

Who may ascend the hill of the LORD?
  Who may stand in his holy place?
He who has clean hands and a pure heart,
  who does not lift up his soul to an idol
  or swear by what is false.
He will receive blessing from the LORD. (Psalm 24:3–5)

I GAVE BIRTH TO FOUR LITTLE SINNERS. THANKFULLY, NOT all at once.

Around eighteen months old, it became obvious that they had come prepackaged with the sin nature they had inherited from me, so right then, I began praying my guts out for Jesus to save their tormented, tantrum-throwing souls. I remember looking at them sometimes and thinking, *Whew, you need a Savior.*

So as the mother of sinners, I am always on the lookout for grace and mercy and kindness. When it happens, I take pictures, throw parties, or haul the blessings down to the convenience store for a round of Icees. It's worth it. I spend way too much time listening to

the sound of my disciplining voice, so I want to remember and celebrate those moments when God seems to take over and turn my
children into loving little people.

AnnaGrace arrived twenty-two months after William. He
smiled but wasn't too thrilled. She was okay, but nothing special to
him. Then one morning, when he was four years old, I walked
upstairs and they were both playing on the floor in her room. I
realized she had on play clothes instead of her pajamas and there
was a diaper beside the door. "William, did you get AnnaGrace out
of her crib?" I asked, afraid to even imagine that escapade.

"Yes, ma'am," he answered.

"Did you change her diaper and put her clothes on?"

"Yes, ma'am," again.

"Oh, William." I picked him up and began to kiss him and hug
him. "What a blessing you are to Mama. Thank you, thank you,
thank you for helping me take care of AnnaGrace."

Exasperated by all the fuss, he said in his best four-year-old aw-
shucks voice, "Mommm, all I did was change her diaper."

That morning seemed like their bonding moment. I thought,
*Those two are going to be best friends. Big brother helps take care of his
baby sister. What a sweet little family we're going to have.* But William's
one act of selflessness toward AnnaGrace wasn't ever repeated. In
fact, I think I made things worse by acting so goofy over him. Soon
after that, William decided that he didn't want anything to do with
AnnaGrace. In spite of all his happy traits, he had acquired one
strong aversion—his kid sister.

He would ask me what kind of cereal she was eating and opt for
the yucky high-fiber over the cool sugary cereal that turns your
milk different colors just to eat something she wasn't. If she was in
the middle seat of the minivan, then he would sit in the third seat
or vice versa. He wanted to be wherever she wasn't. He became

her opposite. And he was mad the day I enrolled her in his pre-school. We'd had one amazing diaper-change morning, and then AnnaGrace returned to her former status in William's eyes—she was the bane of his existence.

That's how things have plowed along with the two of them for the past three years. They live in the same family. She follows him around like a puppy dog. He is annoyed by her presence. I make him give her a hug as punishment for being ugly. He reluctantly tells her, "Friends forever," because I force him to. It's their routine.

Then there was this week. I know it could be an isolated event, never to be repeated, but it gave me hope. I went into the garage and saw the training wheels from AnnaGrace's bike lying there. She hadn't said anything about wanting them off, so I was puzzled about who took them off and why.

Then I saw the two of them out in the driveway. Five-year-old AnnaGrace was pedaling, and seven-year-old William was holding on to her seat and giving her riding instructions. "Pedal faster. Hold up the bike. Don't be afraid." Then he said, "Here, let me show you." She got off and he jumped on her pink Barbie bike to show her what to do. Their big brother, Grayson, was laughing at him for riding a girl's bike. And then William yelled to Grayson, "Who cares if it's pink; it's a really fast bike. You oughta try it."

I stood in the garage dumbstruck. Who was this kid? William had gotten the toolbox down and taken the training wheels off of AnnaGrace's bike. Then he had spent the rest of the afternoon try-ing to teach her how to ride a two-wheeler. The next morning he woke her up early so they could run outside and get back at it.

I felt as if I was watching a mother-dream in Technicolor. My son was loving and serving his sister with nothing to gain. Heavy sigh. It ranks right up there with my dreams of dirty clothes actu-ally finding their way to the laundry room. Homework finished without moaning. Or one of them running into the house to ask, "Would it be okay if I mowed the yard?" Needless to say, these things can be rare in a house with four siblings, but my spirit did cartwheels over one pure-hearted moment.

Looking for a Pure Heart

I realize that William's lovefest may come to an end at any moment, but the lesson of watching him love freely, if only for a few moments, has been good for me. When I began to write this chapter, I came to my computer a bit jaded by old wounds and failures, wondering, *Does anyone ever do anything with a pure heart or with pure motives? What does that look like? Have I had a pure heart for even two minutes?* There is a verse in Proverbs that voices my lament:

> Who can say, "I have kept my heart pure,
> I am clean and without sin"? (20:9)

I don't know about you, but at the end of the day, when I take inventory of my heart, *purity* isn't usually the first word I'd choose. I try; Lord knows, I try every morning, but then the kids come down for breakfast and someone slingshots a waffle across the table and my pure heart evaporates. Truth is, I guess my pure heart can disintegrate several times a day for all kinds of reasons. Maybe you struggle to find pure motives and pure thoughts and pure love inside your heart too.

Babies are great at pure love, but it seems like the older we get, the more the heart gets out of whack. Pretty quickly in life we find ourselves corrupted by that stinking sin nature, our choices, and Satan's work among us. You do realize that you have a bull's-eye on your back where he's concerned. If you love Jesus, then Satan will do whatever he can to get at your heart. He doesn't want you to be blessed or to see God or to know purity. He doesn't want your life to become a beautiful offering.

Over the years, we can figure out how to jockey for position, step around rules for advantage, and manipulate people for gain. We learn to hide and lie and cheat and steal. We can easily begin to live from the contaminated heart, where pride will teach us to think of ourselves above all else.

Of course the Christian woman knows better than to live a blatantly immoral life, so her ugly heart can become cloaked behind pretense, piety, and intricate patterns of pretending. We may have some random moments of purity on our own, but probably not too many. Thankfully, the heart that Jesus is talking about in this passage is the redeemed heart—the one being continually cleansed in His presence, where the change agent, called the Holy Spirit, is affecting our motives, choices, and dreams.

I could look for my pure heart and become discouraged by my own lack and failures. But then I remember that I need a Savior and He is here, and, thankfully, my grubby heart is being made pure every time I humble myself in His presence.

Jesus said to a lot of people on a hillside, and to every follower who has come after,

It is a beautiful offering to Me when you are pure in heart. That kind of heart gives you spiritual eyes to see God.

If you are looking for a pure heart to offer to God, then come with me into His presence and see what happens. The heart finds its cleansing in Him. God does what we could not do for ourselves.

Blind to God

Have you seen God work lately? How long has it been since you really knew that you were being held in His arms? Heard His voice? Watched Him answer your prayers? Are you able to trace His hand across the events of your days? Or do you feel blind to God? One time I heard a woman ask, "If the Holy Spirit decided to leave you, how long would it take you to realize that He was gone?" I remember being convicted by her question and decided that I always wanted to be aware of the presence and power of God in my life. I truly want to see Him.

Sometimes we can't see God because He is teaching us to trust His goodness, but most of the time, we can't see God because the heart has become dusty or cluttered or just plain filthy.

Over and over in the Gospels, Jesus offered His followers "eyes to see." And in this passage, He says that when you are pure in heart, you will see God. The heart can become corrupt over time, or we can choose out of laziness or guilt not to keep it clean. But rest assured, when the heart is dirty, you and I will be blind to God. When a God-follower is spiritually blind, Jesus calls that person a hypocrite.

Woe to You

You remember the hypocrites, don't you? They have logs in their eyes, obviously preventing them from seeing God. They pray in public, long drawn-out prayers, drawing attention to their pious words. They look pitiful when they are fasting so others will feel sorry for them. They make a big deal out of themselves and "do not practice what they preach." Everything they do is done for men to see. They are God-followers with impure hearts.

Jesus got fired up at the hypocrites in Matthew 23 with the

"Woe to You's." He called them blind guides, fools, snakes, and a brood of vipers. He said,

> On the outside you appear to people as righteous but on the inside you are full of hypocrisy and wickedness. (verse 28)

All I have to do is spend a few minutes in that chapter and Jesus gets my attention. He is serious, adamant, repetitive, and bold. He hates the hypocrites who associate themselves with God for their own glory. There are grave consequences for those who become haughty in sin, think more of themselves than they ought, separate themselves out of pride, operate from impure motives, and pretend to be something they're not. Every time Jesus says, "Woe to you" in Matthew 23, I tremble. He's not kidding around.

And we can't kid around either. A part of our beautiful offering to God is to take Him very seriously. We have to pay attention when He is intense about our behavior. He intends for us to represent Christ to the world, and the hypocrite makes Him sick.

Create in Me

Maybe you've felt like a hypocrite. I sure have. Through the years, I've tried to hide my flaws and selfish motives, skirt the truth when I thought it was going to hurt my image or make me uncomfortable. I have pretended that I wasn't struggling when I was. I have let a person think that I prayed for a situation when I hadn't. It's a hard call when someone says, "Thank you for praying," and you realize you never prayed. I don't think I've ever been honest enough to admit, "I'm sorry, but I didn't pray for you." I have just stood there and nodded my head, letting that person think that I did. Hypocrite. Woe to me.

I've done worse to cover my impure heart. But it's never done me any good. Pretending to be something you're not just makes you a big, fat baby Christian. Useless to the kingdom. Immature. Blind to God. I had a professor who used to say that sometimes you meet people who tell you they love Jesus, but you wish they wouldn't tell anybody else. It's not great press for God. They are downright embarrassing. Hypocritical. Haughty. You want to say to them, "Hey buddy, why don't you just keep it to yourself."

> *Pretending to be something you're not just makes you a big, fat baby Christian.*

It's gross to remember that I have been an embarrassment. I ache over that. I long to offer to God an incredibly beautiful life. There were times when I was off and running toward Him with something fabulous to give and then out of nowhere, I'd trip over my laces before I could get to Him. I have been spiritually clumsy. Confession in part sometimes, but not in full. Reluctant or hesitant to ask for forgiveness. Prideful when God was clearly calling for humility. Timid and afraid when He was trying to offer courage and vision. I've had two-left-feet moments and sometimes stumbled over myself, even when I desired to give God something wonderful.

I have always wanted to be a distance runner. Three miles without heaving would be long distance for me. I had tried in the past, but the intense pain underneath my ribs would always sideline me in a matter of minutes. I used to joke that I don't run because I want to be sick when I die. But that was a joke and I still really wanted to run. All my friends run, and it seems like the perfect exercise for a woman who can't find an hour to get to the gym.

So, it finally dawned on me that I probably won't wake up one day and be a runner. Nothing will happen unless I actually get out there and do whatever it takes to become one. About a month ago, I started trying. I wish I could tell you that it happened in a matter of weeks. But I am forty, and becoming a runner is going to take a little more time. I walk fast to warm up, run until that side thing is unbearable, walk it out, and then run a little more. I feel like such a pansy. But if I give up again, I will still never become a runner. I want to run. I have dreamed that I am a runner all of my life. I could quit, but something inside me doesn't want to this time.

The path of my offering is very similar. I want to bless God with my life. I could dream about what God could do with a woman who was devoted to Him. I could talk about being pure in heart. I could intensely desire a righteous life. But until I get my shoes on and try, I will never know the great blessing of running alongside God. Getting your shoes on to try means getting on your knees when you'd rather just run out the door. It means being accountable when it's embarrassing. It means telling the truth to others and to God even when it makes you uncomfortable. Sometimes I will have to press through my fears and respond to God and people with a humbling vulnerability. Running alongside God means that I am learning to confess immediately and cut out the days of waiting for restoration and forgiveness. It means that I try to push through my hesitancy and do the right thing before God. It means that I make an effort to keep asking God to make me pure. There are so many ways that I could spiritually run faster, and I don't want to get older without trying. I don't want to just dream about being godly, I want to keep moving in the direction of God, running *toward* maturity instead of away from it.

This path toward purity is a difficult one. Sometimes we run fast in strength. Sometimes we trip, get turned around, or give up. But the whole idea is that we set our hearts on the Father's love and try.

Just roll out of bed and get out the door and then try. Walking if you have to. Faster when you can. Doing whatever it takes to become a woman with a pure heart.

I can be assured of this. We will never have pure hearts unless we do whatever it takes to consistently get ourselves into the presence of God. If you and I will run toward Him for this blessing, He'll take it from there. Did you know that purity comes from Him and not from yourself? Purity is a gift for your heart, given to those who ask. Running toward His purity means asking God to do what you can't, praying for change in your attitude,

> *We will never have pure hearts unless we do whatever it takes to consistently get ourselves into the presence of God.*

and asking Him to do whatever it takes to clean what has been impure in your life. For me, running toward God means remembering to order my days around His purpose and His perspective. Even if I can't do that flawlessly, I can at least go in that direction. Even if you are huffing and puffing, tripping and tumbling, moving closer to God is the beginning of becoming pure-hearted.

The writer of Psalms begged God for purity like this:

> Cleanse me with hyssop, and I will be clean;
>   wash me, and I will be whiter than snow . . .
> Hide your face from my sins
>   and blot out all my iniquity.
> Create in me a pure heart, O God,
>   and renew a steadfast spirit within me.
>   (51:7, 9–10)

This passage teaches us that a clean heart comes from God. I can't purify myself and neither can you. If the pure in heart are blessed, the amazing thing is that God gives the purity. Whether you are fast or slow. Whether you have a long, beautiful stride or one like mine—it doesn't matter. What matters is that you and I are becoming pure because we are pursuing a vulnerable, honest relationship with the Father.

In a relationship where we are seeking God and He is answering, He is faithful to remove our sin through forgiveness. All you have to do is ask. He gives you the courage to be honest even when it hurts. All you have to do is ask. He exchanges selfish motives for righteousness. All you have to do is ask. He makes your heart pure in His presence. Do you hear this? First, He gives the pure heart to you, and then He blesses your desire for purity with eyes to see His glory.

Abandoning the life of hypocrisy and running toward the purity God freely gives is a very beautiful offering to our Father. In response to your offering, God gives you eyes to see Him.

Behold the Glory

So what happens when we see God? We get to behold His glory! We begin to see Him working in our lives and beyond our circumstances. We can finally make out the lessons He has been trying to teach us for so long. We glimpse a reason for our suffering. We start to envision our purpose in His amazing plan.

A friend of mine is a single mom. Last week her children were away with their dad. She said that loneliness seemed to sneak up on her and finally overcame her in a matter of days. She said that God dealt with her in the pain, and she began to pray and cry more intensely than she has ever known. The wailing wouldn't end. The night was so dark and she had never felt more alone. She became afraid of the severity of her emotions but didn't know what else to do all by herself in her house, so she kept screaming out to God, begging for His presence, His mercy, His forgiveness, His cleansing, and His freedom.

Eventually she had cried herself to sleep but woke in a few hours with a startle. She told me that for the first time in three years, she could see clearly. It all made sense. She could see a part of the plan God was unfolding for her life. She could hear His step-by-step instructions for her own heart and wellness. She felt as if she had answers to prayers she had been praying over her kids.

She had been in the presence of God. He had made her heart pure. Then she got to see His glory. May it be the same for you and me.

Jesus says that the pure in heart get to see God. These human eyes get to glimpse the glory of His work while we are still on this earth. But one day, when we are with Him in heaven, finally made pure for eternity, then we shall see Him as He is. Do you remember what Job said?

> I know that my Redeemer lives,
> and that in the end he will stand upon the earth.
> And after my skin has been destroyed,
> yet in my flesh I will see God;
> I myself will see him
> with my own eyes—I, and not another.
> How my heart yearns within me! (19:25–27)

To finally see God as He is. Sin defeated. My heart made clean. The running finally over. My aching heart yearns as well.

It's now a few days since the bicycle blessing. AnnaGrace wants her training wheels back on, and William has long forgotten that the two of them used to be pals. She came running into the house this morning, crying at top decibel. There were no tears, which is usually an indication that only her feelings are hurt.

In between sobs, I could finally make out the names, "Wi-lli-ammmmm and Gr-ay-sonnnn," so I knew that she was getting ready to rat on the boys. It took a while to get the story out, but it seemed that they had called her Albert Einstein. I was puzzled as to the problem with being called a genius. Sounded like a compliment to me. But it's not a compliment if you have bed head and your hair is sticking out all over the place and your two awful brothers laugh and call you Albert Einstein.

So much for pure-hearted moments. We're back to normal around here with impure hearts and sin natures intact. All five of us have hypocrite potential, and cleansing forgiveness is needed daily.

Thank goodness for a redeeming Savior who came to purify the hearts of mean little boys and tattletale little girls and moms who turn their heads and laugh at Albert Einstein jokes.

Questions for Reflection and Discussion

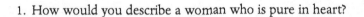

1. How would you describe a woman who is pure in heart?

2. Where does a pure heart come from, and what can we do to pursue purity in our lives?

3. *Hypocrite* is a really strong word. Does it apply to any of the areas of your life? If so, how do you sense Jesus asking you to respond to His call to purity instead of hypocrisy?

4. Does it make sense to you that with a pure heart, you are able to see the work of God's glory in your life? Where do you need to see God's glory? How have you seen His glory in the past?

5. Are you consistently getting yourself into the presence of God? There is where your heart is made pure. Can you make a commitment to be with God every day no matter what? No matter if you're tired or grumpy or distracted or ashamed, your ability to see God depends on your consistent time in His presence. It's beautiful to God that you just show up. He can take over from there. What can you do to improve your consistency?

7

A PEACEMAKER

~

Blessed are the peacemakers,
  for they will be called sons of God. (Matthew 5:9)

You can develop a healthy, robust community that lives right with
God and enjoy its results only if you do the hard work of getting
along with each other, treating each other with dignity and honor.
(James 3:18 THE MESSAGE)

ONE OF THE BEST THINGS ABOUT TRAVELING ALONE FOR
me is the other side of security at the airport. When I get past the
inspection that means everything is done that can be done. The
children are cared for. My bags are packed and loaded. And whatever dust is left at the house will just have to wait until I get back.

My family life is so incredibly loud and crazy that walking to my
gate, with a bottle of water in one hand, pulling my computer
behind me with the other, is one of the most quieting things that I
do. At the airport, I can go to the bathroom and put my lipstick on
straight for the first time in two weeks. I can saunter through the
gift shop and look at all the candy without one of my Can I Have's
asking for anything.

When I'm at home, I instinctively hold out my hands like

guardrails for little people, trying to guide their skipping and walking backward, so it feels weird to walk by myself down the concourse. I always expect to get off balance without a few munchkins attached to my hip. No one spills on me. No one asks if I think an F5 tornado could pick up the jet and carry it across town. No one wants a dollar. And I can read the paper if I want to. Or not. Waiting at the gate is my own personal peace retreat.

I am the girl who craves peace. I pray for it all the time. I will stand on my head to orchestrate peace and do just about anything to restore order. Most of the time, I think everything's going to work out okay. Whatever seems monumental is probably not that important, so we should all be able to get along, find something nice to say, and treat each other kindly.

Last week I was at the airport, fairly peaceful and full of anticipation for the days ahead. We have these wonderful rocking chairs at our little fifteen-gate landing strip, so I sat in one to write in my journal, pray for the children, and think about the conference I was going to be attending. All in all, I was one happy girl, departing for my weekend with a song on my lips and peace in my heart. But as I was about to find out, not everyone else in the world is begging God for peace.

As soon as we got on the airplane, the lady in front of me stood up and yelled, I mean yelled, at my seatmate for touching the back of her hair while putting luggage away. The woman next to me ripped out a slew of curse words, and they were off to the races. A flight attendant had to come and politely ask the ladies to take a seat. More like send them both back to their corners before it came to blows.

I thought, *Wow, the girls in the aisle seats are having a tough day. I'm glad I have peace in my heart.* I sent out a soothing smile intended to make them reconsider their standoff, but it didn't go over too well with either one of them. They weren't ready to smile about anything. They both fumed at each other all the way to Atlanta, and I assume they were probably mad at me for sitting there ridiculously happy in spite of it all.

I had expected a great weekend at the conference. Sometimes it turns out that way. And then sometimes I get home and never want to go back out into the world where the angry people live. The uptight girls on the plane turned out to be a prelude for my days away. There was more in store for me, and the weekend turned out to be very difficult. It seemed as if everyone I met was mad at someone or quick to anger or looking for an opportunity to find fault or feel offended or claim victim status. The worst part is that I was with believers the whole time.

I mean, I can halfway understand two grown-up women without purpose in their lives dueling at sundown over an accidental nudge on the airplane. But what is the deal with the Christians? Why are we acting the same? Tell me what in the world is going on? I am so confused. How can we say that we belong to Jesus and live with such propensity toward anger and rage? Where is the peace, for heaven's sake?

When my children are behind me in the car bickering, I remind them to consider their tones. Then, when they can't seem to restrain themselves, I make them stop talking and tell each one to look out his or her own window. No speaking until they want to sound differently or completely change the subject.

One night we were leaving a friend's house and I had to ask a blatantly disobedient William to walk on the sidewalk through the neighborhood while the rest of us followed behind him in the car. About half a very slow mile later, I rolled down the window and asked if he thought he could ride home in peace. He thought that he could by then.

My kids bug me, but I'm not as frustrated with them. They are kids. Immature. Childish. Prone to tears and frustration. They reach over and hit one another for no reason except that they are squirrelly kids. But I'm really agitated with adults who read the same Bible that I do and still act like my five-year-old.

That weekend at the conference, I had to ask two very grown-up women not to speak to one another until they could change their tones and begin to process without anger. I watched one hit the other. Some other folks got caught in the cross fire of bickering. I heard gossip, slander, and worst of all, someone said to me, "I just want to enjoy being mad at her for a while." Good grief.

I came home so empty. Not peaceful. Restless in my spirit and anxious. Nothing had changed in my circumstances or personal life since I sat peacefully in a rocking chair waiting for my plane, except that I had been with difficult people all weekend. I think I brought them home with me. I came home exhausted and teary. I came home beginning to think like they think.

Paranoid Girl Freak-Out

Anxiety made the flight home with me. Frustration, doubt, and despair were stowaways and came along too. It's now been four days since I got home, and I have prayed for peace and soul restoration ever since I landed. I have walked around this house wringing my hands, lying awake at night worrying and fretting. Feeling sleepy during the day to cope with my fears.

Here's the deal. After interacting with hurt and angry believers all weekend, I came home doubting the integrity of others. I have questioned the motives of people in my life and begun to feel despair, wondering if I'd get hurt if I put my faith into their promises. I was just about to decide not to trust anybody again in some weird effort to avoid the possibility of future pain. But there is no peace in obsessive thinking, and that's what I was doing . . . obsessing over what else or who else might come into my life and cause me pain. The soul is without rest in the spin of suspicion and what-ifs. So, essentially, I spent the last four days a crybaby mess. I imagine that you get the picture.

Believe me, I tried to work it out. I prayed, wrote in my journal, prayed harder, cried, obsessed, and worried myself silly. God waited until last night to break through. Maybe it's because I waited until last night to confess my heartache and finally ask someone for perspective and help. That's when I called Dennis. He is a pastor who has mentored me since seminary, and he knows me well. I spilled out all the potential scenarios regarding my trust and heartache. I told him about the uncertainty in my head. As usual, he listened with great attention and asked thoughtful questions. Then from the depth of his training in biblical counseling and theology, Dennis quickly and accurately diagnosed my heart. "Angela, you're having a paranoid girl freak-out."

Whew. I was so relieved to hear that I wasn't going crazy. This isn't a PMS week, so I couldn't figure out what in the world was wrong with me. I had let the other people I'd been with become loud voices in my head. I let their mistrust become mine. I let their frustration seep into me. I was freaking out over nothing. And all because I let some angry folks steal my peace.

Sometimes it takes me a while. I'm slow. But Dennis helped me realize that this past weekend was a spiritual battle. Satan wants me to live in the land of freak-out as often as possible. He wants me to live underneath the weight of anxiousness and make up things to worry about. He wants me to spend nights without sleep. He'd love for me to crumble into pieces without peace in my heart. And he's working toward the same state of discontent for you.

Satan wants Christians to operate in weakness. He wants us to bicker and argue. He wants to distract us from God. He wants us to mistrust and live with suspicion. Everything about my three days was oppressive and dark. The people I interacted with were underneath their circumstances and angry. No one seemed to be operating in peace or contentment. Maybe they couldn't give what they didn't have.

In Your Possession

It's true, you know. You cannot impart what you do not possess. When Jesus said, "Blessed are the peacemakers," I'm absolutely sure that He knew we must have peace in our possession in order to give it away. We will not be peacemakers until we have become peace-possessors. We have to own it. Live in it. Know what peace feels like.

Where are you in life right now? Feeling complete peace? On a path toward peace? Having a paranoid girl freak-out? Harboring a sense of foreboding and worry? Feeling anger rumbling underneath the surface? Looking for peace in all the wrong places?

> We will not be peacemakers until we have become peace-possessors.

A part of your beautiful offering to God is to have peace in your possession. Peace is an attribute that likens you to God. Remember the last beatitudes about mercy and purity? They also characterize the woman who wants to return God's love with her life. She begins to love as He loves and respond as He would respond. She wants to possess the characteristics of Christ, to have the heart of God inside her to give away.

If you cannot impart what you do not possess, then you and I will have to make a conscious decision to pursue the character of God, becoming the woman He has in mind. Someday, somewhere, you have to decide if you're willing to go for it. I almost remember the exact day that I began considering what it would look like for me to let God radically change my life.

I have to thank Michael Card. He wrote a song that Amy Grant used to sing called "I Have Decided." For me, the life-changing line in the song was, "I have decided to live what I believe." One day I was humming along with Amy and stopped to think about what she was singing. I realized that I was pretty secure in my beliefs. I could have taken an essay exam on believing and passed with great marks, but I had never made the decision to *live* everything I believed. It's a very big deal to believe that Jesus Christ is the Son of God. If He is, and I had decided He was, then everything about my life should reflect that truth. Honestly, my whole life as a believer began to change when I realized that there was a difference between just believing and truly desiring to live my life based on Christ's teachings. It seems so simple now, but it rocked my world then. Sometimes I still ask myself, "Is there anything else I believe that I have not begun to pursue?"

All those years ago, one powerful little song helped me understand that if I believed in God and if I believed that Jesus Christ was who He said He was, then there were no other options than to begin living it.

When you decide that you want peace in your possession, then you want to find out what that looks like and sounds like and feels like. You begin to pray for God to give you peace. You read passages of Scripture about peace. You begin to incorporate peace into your relationships. You decide to respond differently next time. You speak in love. You act in tenderness. You imitate what you know about peace until it becomes a reality for your character and your life.

A Woman of Peace

If you want your life to be a beautiful offering to God, then one of the attributes that He blesses is becoming a woman of peace. Maybe the woman who has become a peacemaker would look something like this:

- She has surrendered her life to God and she's not mad about it. She is learning to trust Him with the outcome and, even beyond trust, she anticipates that His plan will be more exciting and better than she could have imagined.
- She tends the hearts of those she loves. Petty details decline in value. Love matters more.
- She is beginning to see what counts for eternity and gives her attention accordingly.
- She is interruptible.
- She looks into the eyes of neighbors and strangers and the goofy friends of her kids and sees the person who wants to be loved and valued and applauded.
- She understands that life doesn't always turn out right and people don't turn out right and just about everything needs to be covered with forgiveness.
- She is slow to mumble stupid words of discouragement.
- She considers when it is appropriate to become angry.
- She is way past appearances and pretense.
- She surrounds herself with passionate contentment.

Now a quick look at a woman who does *not* have peace:

- She will compromise her offering just to make people happy. She might be a "peaceful" doormat or punching bag or scapegoat.

- She closes her eyes to injustice.

- She is timid and insecure.

- She is a grudge keeper.

- She makes companions of those who lack integrity.

- She runs from confrontation and resolution. Then again, she can be a fighter.

- She looks for the negative in the people she meets and the situations she encounters.

- She is anxious and fearful, looking for disappointment and expecting the worst.

- She is one complaining, whiny-baby person.

- She is prone to gossip and slander.

- She inclines her head toward rumors.

- She might be funny, but she is miserable and leaves you feeling gloomy or sad.

- She is painfully self-centered and easily frustrated.

- She might say that the cup is half empty, with a hole in the bottom, leaking fast.

- She can't see past next week, much less anticipate what might count in heaven.

- The little stuff eats her lunch and derails her attitude.

I think I'd better stop before I really get wound up about women without peace. What I want you to consider is where you are. Are you a peace-possessor? Is there evidence of peace in your life, or is it time to begin living what you believe? How are you at making peace?

Making Peace

I don't think I knew so much about peace before I had children. Moms make peace. It's one of our best things. I am such a peace nut that I am always looking for ways to bring peace into our home. I light candles at dinner around the pizza box. I turn on music in everyone's room in the morning so they can wake up calmly. I try my best to bend down and look into their eyes, especially when I'm redirecting an attitude. I make sure everyone gets quiet time with me before they go to bed at night. Time to speak softly and whisper love and scratch their backs and hug. I want to make peace in our home, but even more I am praying for God to use me to make peace in our hearts.

In my house, making peace might mean explaining why one child gets to spend the night with a friend while the other one isn't quite old enough. It means learning to rejoice over one another's victo-

> *Making peace means that sometimes you have to sacrifice your want-to for someone else's need-to.*

ries without a "Why didn't I get that?" attitude. It means you have permission to say that you are mad or frustrated, but you can't react in a way that hurts someone else. Making peace means that some-times you give up your right to be first, and other times you have to sacrifice your want-to for someone else's need-to. Sometimes mak-ing peace means that you just die to your desire, at least for the moment. The desire to win or hit back or be the loudest or have the last piece of chocolate cake. Funny how you never outgrow the les-sons of peace.

Whether I'm trying to make peace at home or out in the world with the grown-ups, I don't do a very good job when I don't have any peace to give away. The worst days we have as a family are when I am without peace. It's difficult to smooth things out, nego-tiate reconciliation, and realign perspective when I am empty. We all usually know that Mom is completely empty when I scream. I never scream except when I don't have anything left. Maybe it's been a year since I screamed, but it happens. It scares everybody in the house. They move away quietly with wounded looks on their faces. I cry. Then I have to apologize.

I hate it when I am without peace. My kids don't like it so much either. I try not to get there. I try to keep myself in the presence of the Giver.

The Giver

Here is some of the best news I know about peace. Colossians 1:20 says that Jesus

[made] peace through his blood, shed on the cross.

Then Romans 5:1 says,

We have peace with God through our Lord Jesus Christ.

We get to enjoy peace because it has already been made through Jesus, and it becomes a part of our countenance through our intimacy with God.

We could almost put these verses together to read,

Let us keep on having the peace with God that Jesus made for us on the cross.

We do not have to manufacture peace. I think I'd give up if I thought I had to dig down deep and find enough peace to sustain my life. I have peace in my life because I have come to rest in my belief in God. I trust that if I seek His will, He will not hide His direction from me. I believe in eternity, and that gives me peace for these earthly days. I really believe that God works and reworks all things together for good. He restores what has been broken and heals what has been wounded. I don't have peace because I figured it all out. I have peace because I believe in Christ.

Do you remember that Galatians 5 teaches that peace is one of the fruits of the Holy Spirit? That means peace is the by-product of God being set free in our lives. The more room we have given Him to work in our souls, the more fruit we will begin to bear in His name. Peace is one of those amazing gifts that come from being in the presence of God. I can't explain it. I just know that apart from a very real relationship with Him, I have never known any peace. Maybe that's why Paul says in Philippians that God's peace—that soul-settling, I-can't-see-but-I-trust, sleep-like-a-baby kind of peace—transcends all understanding (4:7).

It's always like that with God. We think that somehow we will be able to think ourselves into logical, reasonable stillness of the soul. We wake up in the morning and say something like this: "I am going to have a peaceful day." But we can't. The peace our souls long for was made on the cross and to this day comes only by the poured-out presence of the Holy Spirit in us. It's beyond our human grasp, and yet we get to enjoy the benefits of this supernatural gift. That's called a blessing. You know God is giving peace beyond understanding when the same old thing that always makes you scream happens, but this time you don't. That is a God-given peace that comes from His presence in your heart.

Did you know that God has already set everything up in our favor so that we might bear fruit? He is working for us in this. The scale is tilted to our advantage. He has made the way easy. He carries the burden of providing what we cannot produce for ourselves. He creates the way for us to become peacemakers. I think that takes the pressure off. When I know that I am not at peace, like the past few days, it may take me a while, but I've learned to trust that if I pursue the heart of God, He always comes.

The Family Likeness

Maybe the nicest thing anyone can say to me is that they see Jesus in me. That is the promise attached to this beatitude. When the peace-possessor becomes the peacemaker, then we show the divine family resemblance . . . they will call us children of God. I'd love for my offering of peace to cause someone to think, *She must belong to Jesus.*

Last night I was working and my cell phone rang. It was a local number that I didn't recognize. Always afraid that it could be one of the children, I answered it.

"Hello."

"Hey." It was a man's voice that wasn't familiar, but he seemed to know me.

"Hey?"

"What are you doin'?" he asked like I was his best friend.

I still had no idea who it was, but hoped I'd catch on in a second. "I'm working; what are you doing?"

"I think I might have the wrong number," he said.

"It's a strong possibility," I agreed.

"Yeah, 'cause you sound way too sweet, not like that angry woman I was trying to call."

I laughed so hard and told him, "Good luck with the angry one."

"I'll need it," he added.

Peacemakers. They bear the family likeness. They begin to look and act like God. After a while, they can begin to sound like Him, and even strangers will know the difference. Jesus said that

Your life is a beautiful offering when you are a peacemaker, then you look like you belong to the family of God.

I have to go back into the world next weekend. Airports, shuttles, and two nights at a hotel. For some reason, I think I'm ready to go. It's been a crummy week, you know, the paranoid girl freak-out and everything. I spent four days without peace, and now it seems like such a waste of time. But in the middle of all the heartache, there was a lesson. People can take your peace. They will siphon you dry. You can start out looking like the family of God and end up feeling like an orphan if you forget where peace comes from.

Maybe the next time I begin giving away my peace, I'll remember that I am in danger of running out unless I get myself into the presence of the Giver and ask for more. Then the woman who has peace can become the peacemaker, and everybody will know she belongs to God.

Okay, I think I want to go give the peacemaker thing another shot.

Questions for Reflection and Discussion

1. As you look back over the characteristics of a woman of peace and a woman without peace, where do you seem to be landing?

2. If you cannot give what you do not possess, what does that mean for your spiritual life with God?

3. What do the worst days at your house look like? Do they have anything to do with your personal peace?

4. Does it give you rest to know that peace is given to you by God? You don't have to manufacture it. It's a by-product of being with Him. There seems to be a recurring theme in these chapters. Jesus gives you the characteristics that He will bless if you will spend time in His presence. How does that truth motivate you toward change?

5. What does it mean to you to bear the likeness of God?

8

PERSECUTED

~

Blessed are those who are persecuted because of righteousness,
for theirs is the kingdom of heaven. (Matthew 5:10)

Blessed are you when people insult you, persecute you and falsely
say all kinds of evil against you because of me. Rejoice and be glad,
because great is your reward in heaven. (Matthew 5:11–12)

In fact, everyone who wants to live a godly life in Christ Jesus will
be persecuted. (2 Timothy 3:12)

IF WE COULD SKIP OVER A BEATITUDE, THEN I THINK I'D
like to choose this one. I wanted to tiptoe past these words and pretend I didn't see them. *Oops, we left out persecution. Oh shoot. Well
anyway, let's move along and see what else Jesus has to say.*

But my life wouldn't let me get around this blessing.

I don't remember ever being interested in a happiness that comes
packaged with persecution. I am so conflict avoidant that I never
wanted to know anything about being persecuted for the sake of
righteousness. I just wanted to pray for the persecuted, over there
somewhere far, far away. I only wanted to read about martyrs and
gain inspiration from their courage. I was hoping that I could make

heaven, find my passion on earth, and personally miss this one little *When You Are* altogether.

But there is no such luck. If you are a believer and if you want your life to count for the kingdom, then it's coming. One day there will be persecution and lies and people who want to accuse you falsely, and then you will need to remember what Jesus had to say.

> *If you are a believer and if you want your life to count for the kingdom, then persecution is coming.*

To Look Like Jesus

Just before this sermon, Jesus had been baptized by John and then a voice from heaven said,

> This is my Son, whom I love; with him I am well pleased.

From there He spent forty days and nights fasting in the desert and facing the temptations of Satan. After He had dealt with the accuser, Jesus began to call His disciples and traveled all around the region proving that He truly was the Son of God.

For the first time in all of history, God was on the scene in our flesh and He was delivering on His promise to come to the rescue of His Beloved. The people had to be overcome with great joy and celebration. I can't even begin to imagine what it must have been like to know that you were close enough to touch or be touched by the human hand of God. How humbling and glorious it must have been. There had never been more reason to worship and dance and rejoice than this. Jesus the Savior had really come.

People had been healed, and they were grateful. The possessed had been set free, and they wanted to know how to love Jesus with their lives. Others had been slaves to rules, and now they wanted to worship from their newfound grace. What could they offer? What could they bring that would honor the Son of God?

We know that at the end of any good pep rally, the coach steps up to say a few words. He psychs up the team for the big game, the big fight, and the big win. He might even say, "Win this one for me." But Jesus' words to us are different from the pep talk a coach gives to his players. Jesus might have said, "The battle has been won. The victory is ours. I have come to do all of this just for you." He has already fought in our place and guarantees the outcome.

Our assignment is earth. It's not a game. It's an arduous journey of perseverance and ever-increasing faith. Sometimes it's a marathon and sometimes a full-out sprint. But either way, our victory has been secured. We know who wins. In this sermon, Jesus reflects the heart of God to us and outlines the mile markers for the journey. We can follow these instructions for living, certain that victory is ours and that the race is not in vain.

Our task as disciples is to reflect back to this world the heart, mind, character, and teachings of Jesus. His words to us are more like mission preparation. His encouragement is that there are blessings along the way. He wants us to know that even the encounters that seem like defeat and discouragement can be a beautiful offering to Him.

Maybe in this beatitude, Jesus is saying to us,

It's a beautiful offering when you are persecuted because you look more and more like Me, stand for the things I would stand for, love the ones I would love, and hate the injustice I would hate. I am proud of you when they lie about you and accuse you falsely because you are acting like Me.

And when that happens, then I want you to know that I will draw you deeper into My kingdom blessings.

When He puts it like that, my heart begins to soften and I start to think, *Okay, count me in. If we're signing up for Jesus, then I want all of Him.*

One of the Little People

There are some great books filled with awe-inspiring stories about men and women who have been persecuted and died for their beliefs. In this present day, we know that there are millions of people around the world who are suffering as persecuted Christians. Many are dying horrific deaths in the name of our Lord. I have such great admiration for their courage and boldness. I hold them up as heroes and heroines of our faith. They live shameless, undaunted lives that sometimes end tragically, all in the name of Jesus Christ.

Then there is me. Definitely one of the little people. Just plugging along in my suburban life with my suburban kids. Taylor counted twenty-seven different Bibles in our house last night for some kind of question at school. How cushy is that? I can read the Word of God freely. Worship any way and anytime I please. Talk to almost anyone about the Savior who has come to set men free. No persecution to speak of, and I've really liked it that way.

But there is a persecution that can come to the little people like me and you. It's nothing like the great martyrs have faced, but it is persecution for righteousness, and I believe Jesus gives blessing even in these smaller stories.

I remember losing a boyfriend in college because I was trying to live like Jesus. It hurt for a minute, but it was kind of my fault for hanging around the guy in the first place. I haven't been invited to some parties because people knew I wanted to act like Christ. But that wasn't really persecution, just exclusion. But then there has been the past few years and, more specifically, the past few weeks. I think I have just known a full-blown persecution, and you're going to think I'm weird because even though it hurt so badly, I'm kind of excited about what I've just been through.

A Little Persecution

It seems as if some other folks don't think a woman like me should be allowed to speak for God or about God or about the amazing work He is doing in my life. Last week I was in another city to do a Beautiful Conference. Eight hundred women came, and we met together for three sessions. Little did we know that two church elder boards had been involved for a month with a few people who wanted to make sure the conference did not happen. The spiritual battle had been intense for those men. They prayed for discernment. They made calls to my pastor and elders that I was completely unaware of. They begged God for wisdom and in the end decided that the conference should go forward. No one told me a thing until it was over.

The day I met with the women, God was there to cover us with a thick blanket of His presence. We laughed and cried and sought the heart of the Father together. Our time was amazing. So many have written or called to tell about what God did in their hearts that day and is continuing to do. We were supposed to be together. God ordained each hour. We were blessed and I was very glad.

When the conference was over and my car was packed, I sat down to talk to the pastor who had overseen the event. He decided to tell me about the battle. He told me about phone calls and meetings he'd had with people who didn't think I should be affiliated with God. I kind of understood at first. I didn't know God was going to keep using me either. I didn't know that He would choose to glorify Himself in my brokenness and repentance. But then I heard that their questions had become blatant lies and accusations. They had decided to try to stop our meetings, and their stories to the pastor kept growing.

I wish I could tell you that I was strong when I heard about the false charges and lies, but I sat there and cried like a baby. I ached knowing that godly men had spent so much time listening to these attacks. I felt sick, physically sick, after we finished talking. I can't explain what it feels like to know that a few people are actively pursuing my failure. The pastor called it wickedness and evil. I now know it was persecution.

I went back to my hotel and cried myself to sleep that night. How stupid was that? I had just taken eight hundred women by the hand and walked them into the presence of God. I had told them the truth of my pretending, my brokenness, and God's great mercy and redemption. But when I found out that cowardly people—who had never bothered to speak to me—spoke lies against me, my spirit wailed. I should have been dancing over God's work that day, and instead I was fumbling and weepy and sad.

I drove home the next morning planning my move to Montana. I could pack up the kids, order homeschool curriculum, and get a job somewhere out West as a café waitress. No more telling people about Jesus. No more teaching through the Scriptures. I kept mulling over this plan to run away and hide from the evil. I was so exhausted and weary, and Montana sounded far away and peaceful. I'm sure there aren't any mean people there.

At home I curled up on my bed like a hurt puppy that runs into a corner to hide. God let me cry it out, and then He came to speak gentle words over me.

I think you are beautiful, and I love what you do in My name.

I have you, Angela. You are mine, and I will fight for you.

I see how you spend your time, and I know the intent of your heart.

I have forgiven you.

I have redeemed you.

I am changing you into My likeness.

My name is Perfect Love, and I will battle all the bullies of fear.

I see your scars and your wounds and your mistakes, and I choose you anyway.

Then God reminded me that my work is His. He reminded me about the fruit. The women who stood in line for an hour and a half to cry and tell me what God had spoken to them through our time. The women who drove from Nebraska because this message is radically impacting their lives and their campus. The sixty women who checked a box on a card and asked someone from the church to meet with them.

Over and over, Jesus began to remind me what He was doing through a broken little girl like me. And then He spoke this verse to me:

Persecution for the sake of righteousness is a blessing.

Here is what's so surprising: Instead of sending me to Montana, these attacks have truly driven me deeper into the arms of God. I have found myself in a state of constant prayer, continually checking my heart and my motives, confessing and seeking and studying the Word with renewed passion and fervor. I am certain that God is my safest refuge and He is my strongest defender. I have taught those truths in theory and experienced them in part, but becoming intimately acquainted with the truth of God's protection does something in the heart of a scared little girl. It makes her brave.

I told you that I never really wanted this blessing, and I didn't. But my heart is changing. We got through this round, and I'm not so afraid anymore. Here is what God is doing in my life because of a little persecution.

He affirms that I'm doing something right. If Satan launched an all-out attack against our ministry, then we must be doing something that glorifies Jesus, something that the accuser wants to put a stop to. Hallelujah!

God is using this pain to refine me. First Peter 1:7 says:

These [trials] have come so that your faith—of greater worth than gold, which perishes even though refined by fire—may be proved genuine and may result in praise, glory and honor when Jesus Christ is revealed.

My heart's cry is that my faith would be proved genuine. I may have wanted to momentarily move to Montana, but more than anything I want to live through these trials and little persecutions for the glory of God.

God is giving me another opportunity to radiate Christ. If I can shine for Jesus only when everybody likes me, then big fat deal. But will I bend my knee to these trials with joyful obedience? Will I consider it a privilege to take whatever comes in exchange for the opportunity to share Christ and His love with women all over the country? Everything in me knows this could happen again and probably will, but I'm going to do better next time. I might be stronger. I don't think I'll be packing for Montana. I'll realize sooner that a dark night provides the perfect backdrop for the radiance of Christ.

There are rewards in heaven. My friend used to say to me, "I hope you have a soft seat in heaven." At the end of this beatitude in verse 12, Jesus said,

Rejoice and be glad, because great is your reward in heaven.

In the midst of persecution, we get a double gift—the blessing of being drawn deeper into the embrace of God and the knowledge of rewards waiting in heaven. Wow. So I guess we should return to the Jesus festival. More singing. More dancing. More celebration. If you have known a little persecution because you hang out with Jesus, then maybe there's a soft seat, down close to the front, waiting for you too.

In the midst of persecution, we get a double gift—the blessing of being drawn deeper into the embrace of God and the knowledge of rewards waiting in heaven.

I guess that you're getting to know me pretty well by now. And you've figured out that I have been such a pansy. I would never sign up for even the smallest persecution. I'm not that gutsy, and I am prone to twinges of panic and fear. But God just keeps changing me. I have witnessed, like never before, His supernatural intervention against the forces of evil. He made a way for a woman like me to stand in His name and give out a message of grace. Doggone it, that's the kind of thing that makes you stronger. My responsibility is to remain pure in heart, thirsty for the right living of God, and willing to go wherever He sends me. God has shown me that He is fully able to make a way.

I doubt that you are ready to get in line to volunteer for a little persecution. But will you know what to do when it comes? Will you remember the two promises of Jesus in this passage? Will you cling to the testimony of His protection and be stronger than me while you watch Him come to your rescue?

I think I feel more like dancing today than I ever have. The victory is still secure. The fire was hot and it felt a whole lot like an ambush, but we came through it. I can tell that another layer of fear was burned away. I truly see these tiny glimmers of gold called genuine faith.

The truth is that I would do it all again for the blessing of knowing Jesus more. I witnessed what we were fighting for in the eyes of women who had met with God. I felt myself doing the very thing that I know I am made to do. I hear myself thinking, *Angela, grab hold of something, buckle up, this could just be the beginning. It could get worse before it gets better.* And my heart is pounding. *If this is the only way to go forward in the name of Jesus, then let's go.*

I think my soul just screamed what I have always been afraid to say. "Sign me up for the persecution thing. I'll follow that Man anywhere."

Questions for Reflection and Discussion

1. What is your reaction to knowing that followers of Christ will be persecuted?

2. How have you known persecution in big or small ways?

3. Has persecution caused you to run away from Christ or has it drawn you into a deeper relationship with Him?

4. What have you learned, either personally or from the lives of others you have known, about the blessings attached to persecution?

5. What are the two promises of Christ for the persecuted?

PART 2
As You Go

⁓

JESUS CONTINUES IN HIS GREAT SERMON WITH CLEAR instruction for our everyday lives. I have chosen to call this section "As You Go." In your day-by-day life with God, *as you go*, Jesus instructs you to let these principles guide your decisions and your relationships and your actions.

Right off the bat, I should apologize to the academics. There are a million more thoughts on these beautiful truths. Much more intellectual books could be and have been written. I have chosen only some of the phrases of Jesus to write about, but I revere and honor the whole of His Sermon on the Mount. I wish I knew how to convey the weight of His instruction more articulately. But it's just me. And here is my offering. Some of the words of Jesus. Some of my stories. And prayerfully, some very real application for your life.

In this sermon, we experience the tension between the holy ideals that will never change and never be lowered and the net of grace God provides to catch us. I'd like for you to let your guard down a bit. Be ready to embrace the call to obedience. Anticipate that God just might want to rearrange your whole life around His plans. Try not to shrink back if the Holy Spirit prompts you to reconsider your relationship patterns or your emotional health or your spiritual life with Him.

After the decision to believe on Jesus as the Son of God, the consideration that seems to be most important throughout the Gospels is the direction we face. Are we on the Way? The narrow path? The road less traveled? Are you and I facing Jesus? Are we looking in His direction? Are we running toward His wisdom? His grace? His mercy? And if we stumble, are we falling into His arms?

What I want you to know is that *as you go*, you will inevitably fail. I have. God wants our gaze and our attention, even when we have fallen or made devastating mistakes. Many times in these chapters, I will say something like *Run toward God, Move in His direction*, or *Look for Him.* I want you to learn to think about God sooner and with greater intention. When we have sinned, God wants us to move back toward Him as soon as we realize our error. When life seems dark, let us resist falling headlong into despair. Instead, may we learn to lean into the strength of Jesus as quick as we can remember that His light overcomes every darkness and His strength covers every weakness.

Even in your shame or your consequences or your doubt, God will be blessed if you will incline your heart toward Him. I know too many women who spend half their lives away from God trying to become beautiful enough to be in His presence. It is a beautiful offering to Him that you just come. Don't delay any longer. He is waiting to be with you. Don't continue to hide in your shame. He makes all things new. You don't have to be alone in your pain. He is the Healer, the Giver, and in case you've forgotten, the God of heaven and earth is wildly and eternally in love with you.

I want you to have an intimate, passionate, ongoing relationship with God. I want your life to reflect His love and His grace and His quick forgiveness. I want you to become the woman He dreamed of when He dreamed of you. I want you to know that your life can be beautiful to Him.

I can't think of a more amazing place to learn how to live for God than this great passage. May you hear His voice and return His love with your life.

9

BE THE SALT AND BE THE CITY

You are the salt of the earth . . . You are the light of the world.
(Matthew 5:13–14)

Let your light shine before men, that they may see your good deeds
and praise your Father in heaven. (Matthew 5:16)

MY KIDS GO TO A CHRISTIAN SCHOOL. WE HANG OUT WITH
a lot of believers at Bible studies and church. My best friends are a
very cool medley of godly men and women. And just about every
other weekend I get on a plane to spend a couple of days with a
bunch of women who love Jesus. All in all, my family is sur-
rounded by Christians, all the time, almost everywhere we go. I'm
not sure if it's the best balance of Christ and the world, but it's
how it is for now.

A few months ago I went to a barbecue with one of my children. I'd say which child, but that could reveal too much. The
folks I'm getting ready to tell you about might figure out it was
them and then they could get mad at me. Of course, they might
feel convicted later and actually do something to change their
lives, but I am so conflict avoidant that I'll leave them out of this.
Anyway, it was just me and my unnamed child, and a lot of my

child's friends were coming with their parents. It was supposed to be a party, I guess.

Family by family these people came, out of breath, late, apologizing, grumbling, and carrying a tray of something for the big hoopla. There were all those fake smiles that we pass around at parties Christians come to. Polite conversation without depth or heart. No music. Heaven forbid, no dancing. And miserably, no laughing either. I was just about to die.

So I decided to become the life of the party. It's not my natural role because I am not a true extrovert. But we obviously didn't have any takers that night, and I was going to have to be the entertainment. Let me tell you something, when you try to make people laugh after they have decided in their hearts that nothing in the whole wide world is funny anymore, it's painful. I just wanted to get my kid and my bowl of pasta salad and go home.

I bombed as the vaudeville act, and so I asked Jesus, "Why am I here? This is pitiful. My child is playing with friends, and I am stuck with their dreary Christian parents." I felt as if He told me to pay attention to the women and especially to look into their eyes.

I took my mission seriously and tried to interact with every woman there. I wanted to look beneath the surface of politeness and find out what God wanted to show me. I asked each one a few questions and worked the barbecue the rest of the night. All the women were younger than me, late twenties and early thirties. All of them were tired and burdened. I don't know if one marriage in the room was good, much less great. What came to the surface over the course of the evening was a theme that linked each of these women together. The one thing that I believe God wanted me to see was that every one of those women appeared to have given up.

In her own way, each woman had either gone numb or gone away or gone under. They had stopped calling for help. Stopped trying to figure anything out. Stopped caring what they looked like or sounded like. Timid. Fearful. Guilt-laden. Sad and incredibly without passion. I found myself in a house full of believers desperately without salt and light.

A Salt and Light Phenomenon

There is a phenomenon here in the city of Knoxville. It's called football at the University of Tennessee. I didn't grow up here, and I didn't go to school here, so I don't even know if I can explain to you what happens in this city every fall. People turn orange. I am not kidding. Nobody looks good in that color, not one person I've ever met, but they don't care. Every person in this town wears orange on Friday and Saturday. They fly orange flags on top of their cars and outside their homes. They hang orange-and-white pom-poms from the trunk or the rearview mirror. They paint things orange and grow orange flowers and buy orange beanbag chairs sold along the side of the road. It's crazy.

Yesterday was the first football game of this season. I promise you, I think I was the only person who did not go to the game or stay inside to watch it on TV. I drove to the store and it felt as though I'd missed the Rapture. With 110,000 people at the stadium and everyone else glued to a big screen, this city was empty. No cars on the street. No one shopping. It was weird. They even closed the pool in my neighborhood all day yesterday because of the game. These people are wild and fun and very serious about their football.

Everywhere I'll go for the next few months they'll be talking about the team, make that the only team that matters. They will be so excited that I'll get excited and I'll be talking about football too. I even watched the coach's postgame show this morning because I wanted to catch the highlights and know which plays we'll be discussing this coming week. The enthusiasm is contagious and it lures you in. They make me want to love what they love. I want to go to one of those big parties called a UT game. I might even want to look awful in orange just to be like one of them.

This phenomenon called Tennessee football is salty. It makes everyone who tastes it thirst for more. The orange-colored light called Volunteer-love shines brightly around here. The whole city is attracted to its brilliance, and we instinctively move toward the allure of its glow.

~

So here's my question: Why was the Jesus party with the Jesus people so boring? And why are the Tennessee fans alive and passionate about the ones they love? Something is not adding up here. The UT thing is fun, but it's fleeting. Win today. Yippee. Lose next week. Too bad. But the Jesus thing is eternal. Did anybody hear that? Eternal! And the Jesus thing heals wounded souls and broken hearts. Really, is anybody listening? Call in the marching band. Cue the cheerleaders. We've got even more reason than they do for a celebration. When the Jesus people show up, others should know that tenderness and acceptance just walked into the room. They should be able to "feel" a difference in our spirit and the way we interact. We should make them thirsty for Jesus and the truth of His compassion and forgiveness. We have the opportunity to give Light where they have known only darkness.

Blah, blah, blah. I bet you've heard all this before.

But if you've heard it all before, then why don't our lives look more like orange people for Jesus? When did we stop believing in the power of the Son of God? Why don't our eyes reflect the joy of His presence? How can we withhold compassionate acceptance when Jesus invited everyone to come to Him?

No wonder my neighbors would rather go to the UT game than come to church with me. I kind of understand. Sometimes I'd rather go to the game than hang out with the pretenders and the perpetually downcast. Sometimes it seems easier to cheer for a first down than to cheer for lives redeemed. One time I'd like to show up for church, yell all the words to the fight song, do the wave with my best friends, and cheer for the Jesus victory in people's lives. I know, it sounds wacky. Maybe it's outside your box. God is holy and deserves our reverence. He is and He does. But where have all the salty people gone? Where is the light of the world?

I just don't think we look like what He had in mind. Jesus said, *As you go, be like salt, and as you go, take My light into the world.* I'm not sure what happened to a lot of us. I think maybe we gave up.

Rock This World

I realize that not everyone has given up. I'm not giving up, and maybe you haven't either. I met a woman a few weeks ago who rocked my world and renewed my hope. She owns a secular entertainment business. She was sharp and witty and attractive and more like the salt of Jesus than anyone I have met in a long time.

Every few sentences, this woman filtered our conversation through a verse of Scripture. Every so often she reminded me that she belonged to God and He would give us discernment in our decisions. I was drawn to her. I didn't want our time together to end, and I continue to think about many of the things she said to me. Just being with her increased my thirst for the truth and the presence of God. She is a beautiful picture for me of what I believe

Jesus intended. Since our time together I have thought, *I want to be like the Jesus I see in her.*

Here are the reasons I think that woman is impacting every person she meets with the salt and light of Jesus Christ:

- She continues to take personal steps to become spiritually, mentally, and emotionally healthy and clean.

- She meets with a small group of others who challenge her toward truth and maturity.

- In her failures and in her victories, she is consistently facing in the direction of God.

- She admits her shortcomings and takes them to Jesus. She rejoices in her accomplishments and takes them to Jesus too.

- She takes risks and has found her courage in the boldness of our Lord.

- And finally, this woman would not have anything to give except that she is committed to an extended time, every day, of prayer and study in the Word. She is becoming light because she has been in the presence of the Light.

My new friend leads us in the pursuit of Christ because she is really pursuing Him privately and personally. There is no pretending. Nothing haughty. Just pure humanity seeking pure holiness. I fell in love with her and my Jesus in her.

God is doing something radical and powerful in my heart, and I truly believe He used that woman to begin a new work in me. I need pictures. I need to feel and see. God sent an amazing businesswoman to show me. It was almost like my spirit sighed, "Yes," in her presence. She is showing me what the next step of maturity looks like. I can see it more clearly now.

I want to be a UT football fan for Jesus. I want to rock my world with salt and light, and I am begging Jesus to show me how. It felt as though He said, "Here's what godliness can look like for you. Here's what it looks like and feels like when a strong woman has found her passion in Me."

Ordinary Salt

Jesus turned a corner in His sermon when He transitioned from the When You Are blessings into the As You Go instructions. We are now coming into the specific characteristics that make our lives a beautiful offering to Him. He is speaking to the common people, the "multitudes" who have just been given blessing in the kingdom. Jesus said that these are the ones to whom God gives light and salt. No one has to qualify to be salt and light except that they have divine fellowship with God by faith in Jesus.

When Jesus spoke, the crowds heard about an upside-down world being set right side up. The Pharisees had misrepresented God, and now Jesus had come to set things right. He told us that His followers have markings different from what they have seen or heard. Other people should be able to tell when a follower of Jesus is in the room. In this turning of His sermon, Jesus begins with these words to you and me:

You are the salt of the earth. (Matthew 5:13)

If we are acting like salt then we will affect the world positively in His name. You may have heard some of this before, but it's worth repeating. Let's run through a few of the qualities of salt:

Salt preserves and purifies. Jesus sends us into a world of people whose souls will decay without Him. We are supposed to take the life-purifying message of salvation to them. Salt does not purify or preserve inside the shaker, but only after it has been rubbed into the food. In the same way, in order for our salt to be effective, you and I will have to be rubbed into a dying world, interacting, loving, and becoming right along with them. It's a little scary, especially if we have become the church ladies who live inside the church bubble. But the more excited I get about Jesus, the more I want to be rubbed into the world for His glory.

Salt provides flavor. The application for the Christian is to bring out the God-flavors of this world. Are you looking for the hand of God woven through our days? Do you remind others of His presence, His work among us, and His calling toward Christlikeness? Do others see the person of God because they shared a life experience with you?

Salt makes you thirsty. Do you make anyone thirsty for Jesus? That is so convicting for me. Do people want more of God because of what they have seen and heard in me? Do you remember John 7:37?

If anyone is thirsty, let him come to me and drink.

Our responsibility (as salt) is to make men and women thirsty (for God) because of our lives and then point them to Jesus Christ. His responsibility is to satisfy the thirst.

Salt is a common substance. I am so grateful that Jesus did not say, "You are the gold of the earth," because I'd never think I was ready. But Jesus likens us to the stuff they give you for free in little packs at the fast-food restaurant. I love that. He uses the weak, the foolish, and the despised. Paul wrote in 1 Corinthians,

God chose the foolish things of the world to shame the wise; God chose the weak things of the world to shame the strong. He chose

> *Our responsibility (as salt) is to make men and women thirsty (for God) because of our lives.*

the lowly things of this world and the despised things—and the things that are not—to nullify the things that are, so that no one may boast before him. (1:27–29)

I am just a single mom with four kids. A minute ago, I ran downstairs to make a peanut-butter-and-jelly sandwich for AnnaGrace that she wanted cut into four triangles. After I finish with these words I need to rake the yard because I let the grass get too high before I mowed last night. I fly by the seat of my pants sometimes. I oversleep some days and reach for something chocolate when I'm sad. It's just me, a common woman with a common life. Do you feel common and plain and extremely ordinary? Then Jesus is talking to me and you. We are the ones He has ordained to be salt on this earth. We get to rock this world in His name. God uses small things and small people like us. We cannot let our common lives keep us from this holy calling!

Light on a Stand

Right after Jesus proclaimed that we are the salt of the earth, He said,

> You are the light of the world. A city on a hill cannot be hidden. Neither do people light a lamp and put it under a bowl. Instead they put it on its stand, and it gives light to everyone in the house. In the same way, let your light shine before men, that they may see your good deeds and praise your Father in heaven. (Matthew 5:14–16)

Over in John 8:12, Jesus said of Himself,

I am the light of the world. Whoever follows me will never walk in darkness, but will have the light of life.

It's clear from the Sermon on the Mount passage that the life of a believer is like a lamp or a candle. We cannot *be* the light in ourselves, but we can only reflect to a dark and dying world the light that we have received from the Lord Jesus. Paul said in 2 Corinthians,

God . . . has flooded our hearts with his light, so that we can enlighten men with the knowledge of the glory of God, as we see it in the face of Christ." (4:6 PHILLIPS)

As I see it, there are a couple of poignant applications for us to take from this call to brightness:

A brilliant light is the result of a deeper walk with Jesus. We cannot fake some light for Jesus, although many, including me, have tried. We will not shine like a city on a hill without a close fellowship with God. Because we have an intimate relationship with Jesus, "we see the face of Christ," then God comes through that intimacy to flood our hearts with His light.

I have spoken to this before, but a brilliant light comes from more than just showing up at church or another study. Please don't hear me as knocking church; it can happen there, but it isn't automatic. Becoming the light of the world involves a thirsty, righteous pursuit of the person and heart of Christ.

Pursuing Light gets messy. And it's tiring and sometimes nobody around you gets it. And you keep growing and running while everyone else seems to be spiritually lounging in a hammock, sipping a fruit smoothie, trying to forget the reason they're here. This deeper-walk thing is the only way into greater light. The faint of heart give up. The whiners take their toys and go home. The crybabies blame everybody else for their lack of Light.

Becoming the light of the world means knowing the Light of the World. Seeking the Light of the World. Basking in the Light of the World. You have to get up and get serious and do whatever it takes to get yourself out of the shadows and into the overwhelming, eye-squinting glare of His presence. God is waiting to make you into a brilliant light, but you have to move toward Him in relationship.

The light of Christ in you is not to be hidden. Some Sundays at my church there is so much light in the room that I think we should be able to replace the power grid for our entire city. If that is happening at churches all over the country, then why is the light of Christ so dim in this world? Why is it dark out there? Why are people fumbling their way through empty lives, satisfied with the fleeting strike of a match, when instead they could have the radiance of the Son?

We don't see the reflection of Jesus because people take their light home and hide it. We can sing, "I'm gonna let it shine," all day long and then go right out to the car and snuff it out. What are we so afraid of? Why are we afraid that they'll see Jesus in us? Do we fear not knowing what to say? What to do?

I say to my kids all the time, "Take it to the hoop." They know that basketball term means, "Don't just do a job halfway. Take your dirty clothes all the way to the laundry room. Rinse your plate and put it in the dishwasher too. Clear everything off the table, not just part of it. All the way to the hoop, baby."

I could say to us as the light of Christ, "Be the city." Don't settle for being a twenty-watt bulb, hidden away in some useless closet in the basement when you can be as luminous as the morning sun breaking through the darkness of night. Don't worry about what to say or do or how to respond. The Light-giver will supply every need. Just be the city, baby. Shine the truth of Jesus with everything you've got, and He will focus and refine and disburse your light for His glory.

God seems to be redefining what *shine* means to me. It used to mean quietly speaking into people's lives with Scripture and modeling for them the heart of the Father, as best as I knew how. As I continue to mature in Christ, *shine* is coming to include a compassionate boldness that I never knew I could possess.

> *God loves it when you and I step into the pitch-black night of this world with the candle of His presence.*

As I become more and more confirmed of the truths of God, I am able to give them out boldly. I hear myself speaking in strength to unbelievers, not ashamed of my calling or my Savior. I find myself entering into difficult situations, realizing fully that I am responsible to bring the light of Christ into the room. Through the years and through our relationship, God seems to be turning up the light that He has set within me. Watch and see how He does the same for you.

When you shine, then people get to see the Father. It's true. When folks have been sitting in the dark or hanging around in murky places with dark-hearted people, it's obvious when the light of Christ shows up. God loves it when you and I step into the pitch-black night of this world with the candle of His presence. There is a path to the Father, and your light shows the way.

Jesus said to be salt and light. It's pleasing to Him. It demonstrates to the world whom you belong to. The salty and the light-bearers are becoming a beautiful offering with their lives.

But maybe you haven't made anyone thirsty lately, and maybe your light has almost gone out. Here is the grace of His calling to me and to you:

It's never too late to become.

It's never too late to change.

You haven't been away too long.

His forgiveness can still cover your sin.

His love can heal your wounds.

Your life isn't too broken for Him.

As long as you have breath, it's never too late with Jesus.

He doesn't expect your offering to be perfect. He never said that it would be easy. Move toward Him, and watch Him supernaturally make you into salt and light.

Stay the path.

Let Him pick you up when you've fallen.

Face in His direction.

You may have given up on God, but He has never given up on you.

Go be the city, baby. Go be the salt.

Questions for Reflection and Discussion

⌒

1. Describe a man or woman in your life who radiates the light of Christ. How does that person impact the people he or she comes in contact with? How has the individual's life made you thirsty for God?

2. Do you feel as if you've kind of "given up"? What happened? Where did your enthusiasm go?

3. Do you understand that God is calling us, even in our ordinary lives, to radiate His light into a dying world? Are you motivated or has your light burned out?

4. The thread of becoming like Christ continues in this chapter. What is the key to possessing salt and light?

5. As you consider your life as a beautiful offering to God, how could you grow in these characteristics so that your life is a vibrant reflection of God's love?

10

MAKE EVERY EFFORT

~

Therefore, if you are offering your gift at the altar and there remember that your brother has something against you, leave your gift there in front of the altar. First go and be reconciled to your brother; then come and offer your gift. (Matthew 5:23–24)

Settle matters quickly with your adversary (Matthew 5:25)

Make every effort to live in peace with all men and to be holy. (Hebrews 12:14)

CONFESSION HASN'T EVER BEEN ONE OF MY BEST THINGS.

Hiding sin? I have done that.

Standing quietly instead of owning my faults? Yep, I've done that too.

Repairing broken relationships? It was sometimes easier to pretend that nothing was broken.

Since my childhood, I have known that I am a sinner. I just didn't want to let anyone else in on the secret. I have spent a lot of time acting like, *Who, me? Sin? Nope, never.*

Thankfully, God doesn't settle for halfway. He wants me to keep learning how to incorporate His truths into my character. He wants to teach me about maturity that happens in confession and repentance. He wants the lesson of restoration to begin in my heart. These days it feels as if He is saying to me, *Finally, you're awake and moving toward Me. Let's make up for lost time and lost living. Hey, look at you picking up speed! I'm proud of you. But that's not close enough. Come on; I'm right in front of you. Don't stop short of My glory. Don't settle for less than I planned. All the way, Angela. All the way to the hoop.*

I am a midlife, recovering church lady, and most mornings it feels as though I am only beginning this amazing life of grace that God has invited me to. There is so much more He wants to do in my soul. The past few years of my journey have made me thirsty for Him. I wake up and want to know what I'd look like if God had complete reign over my life. Slowly, but much more surely, I am looking for each next truth that God desires to see reflected in my life.

Our merciful Father keeps moving toward me with the heart-changing power of His Word. I want to give up the woman I used to be and run toward the woman I want to be. When you decide to give up the way you've always been, it's called surrender.

A woman begins to live out the real expressions of confession, repentance, and restoration because there is a divine "giving up" going on in her soul. You know, I've done those things privately and quietly with God all these years, but it's an entirely different gesture to look into the eyes of another human being to confess, repent, and ask to be restored. You may not feel like me, but that kind of humility makes my throat tight. It could make my heart race and my tongue feel like cotton. I could become nervous and anxious and consider forgetting about the whole thing.

But this is how I know that God is growing me up. When my mouth goes dry and my knees feel weak and I think I'll surely die if I have to confess my fault and ask for forgiveness, I am choosing to surrender to obedience and ask anyway. You have to know that's huge for a woman who had grown accustomed to pretending.

An Acceptable Offering

Last week I was running errands like a wild woman, and just as I was about to hop out of the car at the post office, I turned on the radio long enough to hear a man quote from the book of Hebrews. He said,

Make every effort to live in peace with all men. (12:14)

That's all I heard, turned it off, and kept plowing through my list.

A little while later, I was waiting at an intersection when a woman I have known for the past few years drove up beside me. Either she didn't see me or chose not to look at me, but either way, my seeing her was a poignant reminder. I had been in a friendship with her that didn't end so well. I never quite knew where she went or why.

It's amazing how God uses the powerful words of Scripture to stop us dead in our tracks and rearrange our thoughts. Just after I had spotted my withdrawn friend, my head began screaming, *Angela, you are not at peace with that woman and you have to do something about it. Make every effort, remember?*

Not always so quick to obey the promptings of the Holy Spirit, I went to the grocery store and then to the bank, but God wouldn't leave me alone. I was pretty sure that He wanted me to call this woman I hadn't talked to in six months. My stomach hurt while I punched her number into my cell phone. Some days, obedience makes you feel nauseated.

She answered and the conversation went something like this:

"Hello."

"Hey, this is Angela." I tried to muster up some confidence.

"Oh," she said. I knew immediately this wasn't going to be good, but I went for it anyway.

"I'm calling because I just saw you at an intersection about an hour ago, and I felt stupid. I'm calling to see if there is anything I can do to help things between us end differently or better. I don't want to feel stupid the rest of my life, so can we talk about what happened? Can we talk about what didn't happen? Could I say anything or listen in a way that would help?"

"I didn't see you at an intersection," she offered without emotion.

"That's okay, I just want things to be different between us. I want us to be at peace."

"Well, I'm on my way to my son's football game. I didn't see that it was you when I answered the phone. I thought it was somebody else."

"Sounds like I've caught you at a bad time," I said, feeling triple stupid.

"Yeah, gotta go."

"Okay, bye."

Click. No good-bye. No "I'll call you back." No hope that this will ever be straightened out. I could have just about run to the bathroom and lost it. I felt more sick than before I called. And I wasn't too happy with God either.

I mean, I have enough stress. Grayson has an Indian project due with modeling clay and I am not crafty. I have to figure out how to send my taxes to the federal government next month. The hall upstairs needs painting. Every kid in this house needs winter uniforms for school. I haven't spent enough time with the friends that I love, and I've been meaning to bake a pie for my neighbors for two years. Good night. There is enough pressure and guilt in my life to last me decades. I did not need to hear the disheartening voice of a woman who is cold toward me. It ruined my day. What was God doing? And what was I thinking?

I was thinking about these verses. And I was thinking that if I could reconcile with that woman, then it would bless God.

So what now, God? Okay, I remembered someone who had a grudge against me, and I went to her. It was obviously a bust. What do I do with the offering of my life if I have left it at the altar and gone to be reconciled, but she was unwilling? You know, I've tried with her before. I don't think she's coming around anytime soon. So do I just stand here biding my time, waiting for the offering of my life to be acceptable when she changes her heart? Tell me what to do with this verse. Tell me where to go from here.

Maybe you can tell that I was a little miffed with the prompting to call an angry woman. I felt like screaming, "I want my life to be a beautiful offering to You, but I don't know what to do with this!" I think I prayed. I probably whined.

> We can hide from our responsibility in relationships, but God is calling us to move toward the one who is offended or hurt or misunderstood.

But here is the lesson I believe God gave to me. There are three instructions for us in these verses:

First, *acknowledge your sin to yourself and to God.* When you and I remember that there is someone who has a grudge against us, it is our responsibility to own the part we play in the disagreement, misunderstanding, or conflict.

Second, *move toward the person.*

We can hide, cover, or run from our responsibility in relationships for the rest of our lives. But God is calling us, very specifically in these verses, to move toward the one who is offended or hurt or misunderstood.

Third, *go immediately*. That means pretty soon. You know, right after it has come to your mind. Waiting three years is not immediately.

My daughter was in the car with me and she had just had an encounter that was difficult. I said, "Call that person right now and try to make it right."

She said, "I don't know if I can."

"I know it stinks, but one of the characteristics of a Christian is that we try to resolve quickly," I offered.

"Did you just make that up?" she asked.

"Jesus made it up and said, 'As you go, look like this.'"

"Sometimes this is hard," she mumbled as she reached for her cell phone.

"Most of the time, this one is hard for Mom too."

Days went by and I continued to reflect on my desire to live these verses with my grumpy friend. I decided that I had followed the instruction, even though reluctantly. We just didn't get to the reconciled part. And honestly, unless she comes to a softer place, there might not ever be reconciliation. I felt so stuck about what to do with my offering. Can I still bring it to God if we don't ever reconcile?

Then I remembered the Hebrews passage on the radio that had initially prompted my call. The writer had said, "Make every effort." When I put these divine words from God together, then I get,

> Make every effort to acknowledge your own sin.
> Make every effort to move toward the injustice.
> Make every effort to reconcile immediately.

That's all we can do. Make every effort to honor the words of Jesus. Check your own heart. Respond in obedience. And then rest. I can only be responsible for me, and you are only responsible for you.

A man I know wrote down the three things he was most thankful for. After God and family, he said that he was thankful for a clear conscience. His gratefulness spoke to me. When you and I have made every effort in a relationship, then we are clear, the heart is pure, and the offering is acceptable.

Obedience Inside the Net of Grace

Before we move on, I want to take a few minutes with the call to obedience.

> If you are going to "make every effort" in your relationships, then obedience will be required.

If we are going to be faithful to confess, repent, and reconcile, then we have to learn to respond to God out of obedience. If you are going to "make every effort" in your relationships, then obedience will be required. This part is hard and the spirit can easily resist. Most of the time, it's just easier not to obey. Obeying involves a surrender that seems unfamiliar to us. We have become excited about the fresh teachings of God's grace and grabbed hold with lots of gusto, but in the process, many of us have turned away from His call to obey. The Sermon on the Mount is not unclear. Jesus very methodically instructed us to put on His teachings as an act of obedience to God. He called our obedience a beautiful offering of our lives.

There is no easy way through this text called the Sermon on the Mount. Jesus unfolded for us the inflexible, ideal absolutes of God's calling in our lives. These are the everyday living instructions for ordinary people who love God. He revised the laws of the Old Testament and expanded their latitude. He called us to nothing less than God imitation when He said,

> Be perfect, therefore, as your heavenly Father is perfect.
> (Matthew 5:48)

Most of my life I have felt the heavy weight of this sermon like a noose tied around my neck, ready to hang me for my next act of disobedience. Year after year, encounter after encounter, I keep coming to the same conclusion: I want to. I am trying, but I am unable. I talk with a lot of believers who feel the same way. Some are ready to give up on their faith because their obedience has been inconsistent. I want you to hear the call to obey couched inside the heart of God's grace and compassion for you.

I think that many of us have heard only half of the story. We've listened to some well-meaning expositor butcher the text, flog us with the application, and then send us home feeling guilty and hopeless. So we gave up on applying the Bible to our lives or we kept up with what we could and skimmed over the parts that made us wince.

Jesus did not give us these words to hang us. He gave us these words to tell us about the character of God. When we choose to follow Christ with our lives, the call to us is toward His likeness. He wants us to reconcile our anger because He does. He wants us to protect life and marriage because He does. He wants us to keep our oaths to be like Him. He wants us to love our enemies because of His love for them. And He calls us to perfection because that's the very essence of who He is. He can't and won't lower the bar of His character just to let us feel better about our lives.

Jesus did not make this turn in His teaching to throw us into despair or to take away our hope. He spent a huge amount of time in the Gospels establishing the ideal for our lives. The standard. The goal. The mark. But this was not His way of encouraging more legalism. The Pharisees had already concocted enough to go around.

And so, the only way to resolve the balance between the extraordinarily high ideals of Jesus and the disappointing reality of our ability to measure up is to realize that we can't. Even more profound is knowing that we don't have to. Make sure you hear this. Perfection is a lofty aspiration. God asks you and me to run toward it with our lives, but He knows that we can't get there, and what's more amazing, we don't have to.

You can take a deep breath now. Remember a few chapters back when I said there is a reason that we need a Savior? Same truth holds here. God has outlined His unchangeable, holy standard. It reflects to us the sacred attributes of His person. Our God is holy and perfect and almighty. That's why He deserves our worship and the beautiful offering of our lives. But He knew that we couldn't be perfect, so He sent Jesus as our Savior.

I really want to make sure that you understand this sweet balance of truth before we press on, so I want to give it to you again in a few bullet points:

- God is perfect.

- In this sermon Jesus gives us the attributes of a life lived as a beautiful offering to our perfect God. The attributes are taken from the characteristics of His nature.

- You and I are called to live our lives so that we might reflect to the world the character of God.

- But God knows that it's just us, humans beings, made from dust, who will never be perfect.

- And so, He covers us with the righteousness of Jesus and holds us with the goodness of His grace.

- Our assignment is to live from obedience, pressing toward the mark of God's standard. Our blessing is to live grateful for the net of grace where God catches us when we fall.

If these ideas get inside of you and settle deep within your heart, then you get to live your life with great joy and freedom—a happiness that I believe reflects the desire of our Father in heaven. There is plenty of heartache and suffering and sadness in our lives, but there is an abiding joy that comes to the woman who is living with a desire for obedience, knowing that she is held by grace.

If you miss this simple, yet profound balance, then you can still make heaven. But you might go there as a legalist who spent her life keeping rules and doling out judgment. It's a miserable way to spend the gift of your years. I think God envisioned more. I think Jesus taught a better way.

At the end of the day can we ask ourselves, "How did it go with me and God today? Did I make every effort? Did I desire His character? Did anyone see Jesus because of me?"

Every once in a while the answer will be yes. Most of the days, I lay my head on my pillow and think, *I gave it my best shot. I ran in the right direction. I wanted to be more like Jesus. But I tripped a few times. I came up short. I could have done better.*

After one of those quick nighttime checkups, I used to lie there and fret. Now I am learning to hand the offering of that day to Jesus anyway.

My daughter Taylor is a straight-A student in her heart. It's just that she is social. So we don't see too many straight A's. I keep asking for A's because her mind has the capacity. But most of the time, she'll ask me to sign something less. When I look at a paper with a 78 or an 82, I'll find what's good, give her a few pointers on the other, and then say to her, "Did I tell you that I love you today? I want you to do your best because I love you, and I want you to rest tonight because your mama will always be crazy about you."

Sometimes I imagine God saying the same thing. "My love for you is unchangeable. I want you to keep trying because I love you, and I want you to remember that no matter what, I'll still be wild about you."

Then I can sleep without anxiousness or worry. I may have handed God a paper with a D+ on it that day, but His grace wraps me in the quilt of His love and whispers, "You get some rest now. We'll get back out there tomorrow and give it another go."

———

Remember the episode with my grumpy friend? When she drove past me, the Holy Spirit prompted me toward obedience. I shuffled around, but eventually made the call because I wanted to be reconciled with someone who seemed to have something against me. My words were not flawless. The outcome certainly wasn't perfection. But I think that God was pleased because I desired to live by the teaching of this sermon and actually dialed her number.

Obey as Jesus prompts your heart, do everything you can to put on His principles for living. Sometimes your offering will be near flawless. And sometimes your offering of obedience will be an imperfect effort, acceptable because you are caught in His net of grace.

Questions for Reflection and Discussion

1. In the Sermon on the Mount, Jesus gives us everyday living instructions for life. What does the instruction to be reconciled with your brother bring to mind for you? Is there a relationship in your life where this truth can be applied immediately?

2. When I bring up the idea of obedience, how does that settle with your spirit? Do you feel yourself getting angry and decide not to try because you've had so many failed attempts, or can you embrace the idea of obedience as a characteristic of your beautiful offering?

3. When I tell you that God will not lower the bar of His perfection and then Jesus calls us to be perfect as He is perfect, what do you do with that? How does your heart respond to this high call toward holiness?

4. Do you feel you live a balanced life—the pursuit of obedience and yet grateful for the net of grace?

5. As you look back over your spiritual life, do you see a woman who is learning to respond to God's truth more quickly, a woman who is being changed into the likeness of Christ, or do you see a woman who has gotten stuck along the way? How is God prompting your spiritual life now?

11

KEEP A SECRET LIFE

—⁓—

*When you give to the needy, do not let your left hand know what
your right hand is doing, so that your giving may be in secret. Then
your Father, who sees what is done in secret, will reward you.
(Matthew 6:3–4)*

*When you pray, go into your room, close the door and pray to your
Father, who is unseen. Then your Father, who sees what is done in
secret, will reward you. (Matthew 6:6)*

*When you fast, put oil on your head and wash your face, so that it
will not be obvious to men that you are fasting, but only to your
Father, who is unseen; and your Father, who sees what is done in
secret, will reward you. (Matthew 6:17–18)*

MY TEN-YEAR-OLD NEPHEW, SIMON, TOOK HIS PARENTS TO
school for open house. You remember how those go. The classroom is newly decorated. The parents sit in little chairs. And the
teacher talks to everyone about assignments, grading, and expec-
tations for the coming year.

In Simon's class the teacher had asked her students to write the
answers to a few questions in a notebook for the parents to review.

One of the questions was about a wish coming true. Another was about becoming a grown-up. And then there was this question: "Who do you belong to?"

Some of the kids responded with the expected things. "I belong to my parents" or "I belong to a family" or "I belong to the Boy Scouts."

Simon wrote, "I belong to heaven."

His answer takes my breath away and makes me cry at the same time. My little soccer star nephew knows where he belongs. Wow. I love that so much.

When I was ten, I didn't know for sure that I belonged to heaven. I was afraid that one wrong move could keep me out. Can you imagine what a difference it will make in Simon's life because that truth is already settled in his soul—he belongs to heaven?

Jesus said that when we have called Him our Savior, then we belong to heaven too. It's our home, the kingdom of our citizenship, the place our hearts long to be. In these passages, we're studying the kingdom culture. What do the people who belong to heaven look like? What language do they speak? How do they go about their lives? What are the distinguishing features of a man or woman who belongs to the God of heaven?

In the first eighteen verses of Matthew 6, Jesus says that when we belong to heaven, God wants us to have a secret life with Him. Sometimes we are living right out in the open like a city on a hill, but the fuel to burn brightly comes from the secret life we begin and maintain with God.

In His Arms

There is something about this instruction that connects with my heart. Maybe it's because most of my life is lived so publicly and my writing is fairly vulnerable. Maybe it's because I always have a lot of people in my house or in my car or in my Day-Timer. Maybe it's because I am really an introvert who longs for intimacy and reflection. I'm not sure, but I truly delight in remembering that God wants to meet with me in secret.

When I think of my secret life with God, I picture myself in His arms, comforted by His merciful forgiveness, strengthened by His words of encouragement, and close enough to understand His desires for my heart. I imagine myself, a little girl on his lap, being calmed in His presence, laughing and interacting, then sitting quietly in the security of His embrace.

I know this is going to sound girly, but every time I close my eyes and picture myself in the arms of God, I cry. I think I cry because I envision the arms of God protecting me, and I am relieved to remember His strength when I am weak. When I close my eyes, I see that I really do belong to Him. No matter what comes to me or doesn't, I still belong to the Lord God Almighty, the King of heaven and earth.

Maybe I cry because sometimes I'm afraid to be all grown-up and alone, but in my secret place with God, I remember that I am never alone.

And maybe I cry because my joy is so great. Heaven. I have a place there and I'm sure of it and nothing can ever take that away.

But when I have forgotten to come in secret to my Father, then I can forget where I belong and whose I am and where I am going.

Keeping the Secret

One of the main points that Jesus wanted to drive home in this text is that He doesn't want us to make a performance out of our relationship with Him. He calls the ones who "do acts of righteousness" in public *hypocrites.* And He says that if you give or pray or fast so that other people will notice, then that's fine; enjoy your applause, because that's all you're getting.

Jesus is the only One who uses the word *hypocrite* in the New Testament, and He does so seventeen times. The classic Greek definition is "an actor, such as one on a stage." It can also refer to one who practices deceit. The emphasis here is on the intent of the heart. The question is not, *Are we seen doing a good deed?* but, *Are we doing a good deed or praying or fasting in order to be seen? Are we acting devout just for the approval of others?*

There are a couple of things that really matter to Jesus in this passage. One is the real intention of our hearts before God, and the other is that we learn to practice a secret life with Him. He instructs us to *give* in secret. *Pray* in secret. And *fast* in secret. Jesus is very specific here. And so we have to let each of these disciplines have its proper weight and importance. These traits are significant components of the life God wants for you.

It is a beautiful offering to make this journey with a part of your life reserved just for Him. There should be elements of you that no one else knows about. There are spiritual acts of worship being offered only before the private audience of God.

I don't know if this inspires you, but I totally love this. I love that God wants a secret relationship with me. I crave intimacy, and this is just about as intimate as it gets. Three beautiful pieces of our lives, seen only by the Father. Three acts of service, offered in private, that get the attention of God. He holds these attributes in such high esteem that He promises to reward our lives when we're keeping the secrets.

Giving in Secret

But when you give to the needy, do not let your left hand know what your right hand is doing, so that your giving may be in secret.

Then your Father, who sees what is done in secret, will reward you.
(Matthew 6:3–4)

When your life is becoming beautiful to God, He says that good deeds of giving will begin to naturally flow from your character. In fact, the person who is being transformed into His likeness gives so readily and easily that she hardly reflects on what she is doing. They barely notice their own good deeds and they rarely remember them. For that person, it would feel like the left hand doesn't know what the right hand is doing. Giving becomes "no big deal" for the one who is learning to give in secret and without regard for attention or approval.

The question for all of us is, "How's your giving in secret going?" I know. I could get so convicted here. I remember to do it sometimes, and then I'll go along for a while hoarding everything or giving for the wrong reasons. I can forget how much it blesses God for me to give like this. So here's the idea. We have to practice giving in secret until it becomes a part of who we are. We have to remind ourselves until we have learned to respond from our abundance. And we have to do all this in private.

So let's begin today. Do you have twenty dollars, an extra casserole in the freezer, or a bouquet of wildflowers you could gather? Ask God to direct you to the need. And then take great pleasure in the joy of secret giving.

As you and I begin to grow in the discipline of quiet giving, God has promised to reward. I imagine that a part of His reward to you will be an extra provision of His resources, energy, and joy. As you give, He will provide more to give. He will increase your desire to give. And the joy you come to know in this secret discipline will be multiplied by His joy over you.

Over the past couple of years, I have gone to the mailbox a few times and found an envelope of money, usually about a hundred dollars. It's always in cash and always without a note. The envelope has a scribbled "For Angela" on the front. I have no idea whom to thank, so I thank God for the one who has been giving to our family in secret. I ask for God's continued blessing on that generous heart. And I pray for an opportunity to give to someone else in the same way.

Praying in Secret

Matthew 6:6 reads,

> But when you pray, go into your room, close the door and pray to your Father, who is unseen. Then your Father, who sees what is done in secret, will reward you.

I have a friend here in town that designed and built a new house a few years ago. Their home is fabulous with large rooms, a spectacular view, and very thoughtful attention to the details that reflect the personality and needs of this particular family. One of the details that I think about often is the mom's decision to incorporate a prayer closet into the hallway of the downstairs.

It's a tiny little room, and I mean tiny. There is just enough space for one person to lie down or kneel. There is an electrical outlet for a lamp and a shelf to hold a Bible, a journal, and a few books. On the wall are pictures and Post-it notes of prayer requests and Bible verses. Before the carpenters finished the drywall, the mom went to this roughed-out room and put her favorite verses on the studs that surround the tiny prayer closet. And now, when she goes there to pray, she usually finds scraps of paper lying on the floor. They are the prayer requests that her kids and husband leave for her.

Don't you love that idea? I think it was brilliant. And I especially love that the children are growing up accustomed to prayer being central to their lives, so important that a room in their house is devoted to prayer.

I'd love to have a prayer closet. But I don't. I don't even have a walk-in closet anymore where I could push the shoe boxes around and make room to be in there by myself. I just have a bedroom that everyone else thinks belongs to them too. I close the door but decided not to lock it a long time ago. I don't think we've ever had an emergency, but I always want the kids to be able to get to me. So what's a woman to do without a prayer closet and very little privacy? Pray anyway.

Sometimes I get up early and pray without so much as a peep from anyone else in the house. Sometimes I get up early and one by one they will walk in on my praying forty times to ask for breakfast or tattle or just stand there and look at me. Sometimes I hear them searching for me out in the hall and talking to one another. "Mom's praying," one of them will say in the same way I've heard them say, "Mom's taking a bath" or "Mom's working." That matter-of-fact tone in their voice makes me smile to God.

In this season of our lives, time alone to pray is a rare commodity. I don't know of anyone who just has loads of time to be alone with God. What that means to me is that we'll have to be creative and bold and give serious attention to this instruction. Jesus very specifically calls us to a secret prayer life with Him. That doesn't preclude us from praying in public or having prayer partners or maintaining a prayer life with our families. But this passage is difficult to misinterpret. It is a beautiful offering to God when we have a secret prayer life with Him.

There are such great books out there on prayer. There are prayer journals, prayer calendars, and probably DVDs that will give you step-by-step instruction in regard to prayer. In this passage, Jesus gives us a model of prayer that we know as "The Lord's Prayer," and all throughout the Scriptures, we learn more about how and what to pray.

I don't mean to make this too simplistic, but I don't believe *not knowing* how to pray is the greater problem. It seems like the problem is that we just don't pray so much. Maybe we shoot up a few *bless me* prayers or *forgive me* prayers or *help me* prayers, but that's not the kind of praying Jesus is describing here.

Prayer-closet praying is extended. A significant slot in your precious day-planner is cleared for this discipline. You are alone and quiet before God. The prayers are intimate and personal and vulnerable and searching. You might be on your face lying reverent before Him or standing with arms outstretched in desire for Him. You get better at praying in private because you keep coming back in practice.

I guess if I could give you only one spiritual gift, I'd give you a powerful prayer life. When I ask God for spiritual strength, I ask Him to make me a woman of great prayer. You and I will come to know the Father, the heart of His love, the bounty of His grace, the clarity of His will, and His plans for our lives, not because we stumbled across them or fell into them, but mostly because we have been alone with Him in secret prayer.

Fasting in Secret

In Matthew 6:17–18 you will find,

> When you fast, put oil on your head and wash your face, so that it will not be obvious to men that you are fasting, but only to your Father, who is unseen; and your Father, who sees what is done in secret, will reward you.

Sometimes when I am writing I "fast a chapter." I just leave off solid food until the chapter is done. It's not forty-day fasting, and it's not incredibly hard to do. But for the girl who likes to keep a box of Lucky Charms cereal close by, it's significant.

I write a million times better and faster and with greater clarity in the process when I'm fasting. I don't know if the words are any better, but it's so much easier in my spirit. And with that said, you'd think that I'd drop-kick the Lucky Charms every single time I write. But I don't. At least I haven't always done it in the past. I am learning to do it now. Here's why: In this secret discipline, God does something that I can't even describe to you. I have more energy. I am more motivated. I have greater desire for His pleasure. And wouldn't you know it, the chapters that I get the most e-mails about are usually the chapters during which I have fasted.

To fast in secret is akin to knowing something that no one else knows. It's very cool to have the interaction of fasting with God in private. It is affirming in your spirit to be without food and yet sense the strengthening presence of God, both in your body and mind.

Sometimes it takes me a while to catch on. But Jesus knew what He was talking about. When we are fasting for the purpose of connecting more deeply with the heart of God, then He comes to sustain our body and soul with the invisible rewards of His kingdom.

Perhaps the greatest blessing to come from keeping a secret life with God is that we are free from the control of others' opinions.

⌒

Perhaps the greatest blessing to come from keeping a secret life with God is that we are free from the control of others' opinions. We are not enslaved to their approval. I love that when you give in secret or pray in secret or fast in secret, then your motives are made clean. You act in obedience to please your unseen Father. You respond with a pure heart, solely as He directs you in private. And the rewards He gives are the intimate gifts of a loving God for His beloved.

> *God rewards the secret life with a God-confidence.*

In the secret place we can bury ourselves in the robes of God. We can be renewed and strengthened by the covering of His glory. We can hide underneath the shadow of His wings until we are healed and secure in His love. God rewards the secret life with a God-confidence. The woman who maintains this intimacy with her Father learns to interact with the world from the security of her relationship with God.

In the secret place, God whispers until we remember, "You belong to heaven. No one else can have you. No enemy can overtake you. No temptation will overcome you. No disease will destroy you. It is sure. It has been decided. You belong to Me."

Questions for Reflection and Discussion

1. When you close your eyes and think about your secret life with God, what do you see?

2. How does it make you feel to remember that God wants a secret life with you?

3. What about the practice of giving, praying, and fasting in secret? Privately access your secret life and ask God for His encouragement and direction.

4. Is it possible that you lack a God-confidence because there is very little that is secret or intimate about your relationship with God? What areas of your life require more confidence than you currently possess?

5. How could you begin to give priority to the aspect of your life that only God will see? Remember that God rewards your secret life with Him.

12

STOCKPILE IN HEAVEN

~

Do not store up for yourselves treasures on earth, where moth and
rust destroy, and where thieves break in and steal. But store up for
yourselves treasures in heaven, where moth and rust do not destroy,
and where thieves do not break in and steal. For where your trea-
sure is, there your heart will be also. (Matthew 6:19–21)

In his great mercy he has given us . . . an inheritance that can never
perish, spoil or fade—kept in heaven for you. (1 Peter 1:3–4)

WHEN I WAS IN COLLEGE, THE UNSPOKEN MOTTO THAT
seemed to be woven through every class of each semester was "Do
whatever it takes to accumulate."

Accumulate knowledge.

Accumulate strategies.

Accumulate social status.

Accumulate wealth.

Accumulate power.

And then, finally, if you're really lucky and play your cards right,
after having done all of the above, you will accumulate happiness.

It might just take me the rest of my life to unlearn most of my
expensive education.

Let the Unlearning Begin

When Jesus began His public ministry, the first thing He said was,

Repent, for the kingdom of heaven is near. (Matthew 4:17)

The crowds came to the hillside that day to hear about the nearby kingdom. Instead of detailed kingdom descriptions, Jesus talked to the people about a lifestyle. He described for them and for us the lifestyle of those who want to live in the kingdom of God.

Over the course of His ministry, Jesus had this amazing way of turning everything upside down:

You have to lay down your life to find it.
The smallest shall be the greatest.
The first shall be last and the last shall be first.
The ones who give are actually the ones who receive.
When you give up, then you can be saved.
Freedom comes to those who yoke themselves to Christ.

And now, He says that you have to let go of your treasure on earth in order to have treasure in heaven. It goes against everything we've been wired to think. We are accumulators. We measure the worth of a person by the size of their stash. We hoard stuff. We save for rainy days. We spend what we don't have in order to feel that we have enough. And we sacrifice our integrity in order to have more. Living this instruction is going to require us to unlearn the foundational elements that many of us have built our lives upon. I know that sounds dramatic, but I'm not exaggerating. This stuff is deep in our fibers.

There is a bit of rebellion that goes on in our minds when we begin to lean into Jesus' upside-down teaching. We have not understood the heart of the Father, and so our old ignorance about the character of God fears believing.

We are afraid that if we fully give ourselves over to the will of Christ, then He will surely require the very thing we hated to consider. I've probably heard a hundred people say, "I was afraid that if I told God, 'I'll do anything You ask,' then He would send me to a jungle to be a missionary." And I think in these verses, that same kind of fear screams the loudest, "I am afraid that if I unclench my hands from my treasure, then God will take it all away."

We know so little about the heart of the Father.

Where Your Heart Wants to Be

How about if we begin with the end of this passage and work our way back to the beginning? If Jesus says that your heart will end up where your treasure is, then where do you want your heart to be? If you can decide where your heart longs to be, then I think we can get this one figured out.

According to these verses, your heart has two options:

1. Your heart can belong to heaven and the eternal riches of the kingdom. That means that you begin to treasure the same things that God does.

Or

2. Your heart can belong to the earth and the possessions you have accumulated. All that stuff, by the way, is doomed to decay or thieves or it will eventually be taken from your grip in death.

Here is what you have to understand. You can belong to Jesus, be saved and set apart for all eternity, but still not have a kingdom heart. You can know and believe what the Bible says, but never make the transition into actually living these truths.

I have a friend who teaches me so much about where my heart should want to be. Maybe more than anyone I've ever known, this man and his wife truly have kingdom hearts. They have taught their children the same. Their whole family lives with a great awareness of God and a deep appreciation for His goodness. I love to be with them because they see the blessings. They value the riches of the kingdom. They receive the gifts of our gracious God with obvious rejoicing and praise. Little things are big to them. Freshly baked bread is a treat to celebrate. A camping vacation is akin to a cruise in the Caribbean. Having free tickets to a local theater becomes a party. I don't think I have ever heard anyone in that family ask, "Why didn't we get more? Why do others have something we don't? Or what can I do to be like them?"

Maybe what's even more powerful is to watch them celebrate the riches of the kingdom. When a stranger comes to Christ, they cry and dance and thank God for days. They sacrifice on clothes and having the latest, greatest so that there is more left over to give away. I don't ever remember a time when someone in need wasn't sleeping on their couch. Most of us think we have to have a guest room with a private bath to take someone in. This family just has to have room on the floor. They give away their food and their cars and their money. They stay up late praying with anyone who knocks on the door. They welcome everyone and judge no one. I go to their house on the other side of the country every chance I get. I just want to hang out with people who know more about the treasure of heaven than I do.

They love life and love God and rejoice in their kingdom

inheritance. I love being with these friends because their under-standing of treasure keeps transforming my old accumulate atti-tude. I like what it feels like to think as they think. I desire to see the treasure that they see. I want to operate in the same con-tentment they know. In their family, the journey has become less important than the people they meet on the way. The goal mat-ters, but honoring God in the process matters more. Maybe more than anyone I've ever met, this family is teaching me to stockpile in heaven.

Relearning to stockpile in heaven will be huge for most of us. It will probably require a radical change in our thinking. But first you have to decide where your heart wants to be. Will you merely lis-ten to the Sermon on the Mount and nod your head in agreement, or will you begin to put on its truth, so that the teachings of Christ affect the way you value things?

If you want to redirect your heart, then lead with your treasure. Choose what will matter more to you, the earthly accumulation or the kingdom wealth. Decide where your riches will be stored, under your mattress or in the safekeeping of heaven. If the heart follows the treasure, then where will your heart end up being?

A Kingdom Heart

Not so long ago I was having dinner with some women at the Rescue Mission. There was a woman who sat across from me most of the evening. She came to the mission only at night and spent her days walking around downtown, going to the library when it was cold. She was in her early fifties, but looked as if she was in her sev-enties. She had been unwanted as a child and forced to take care of herself since her early teens. Street-educated. Homeless. And without anyone to call family, this life from mission to mission was the only one she had ever known. All her earthly possessions fit into one small duffel bag.

We had a sweet time at dinner, and then she leaned across the table to ask if she could tell me something.

"Sure, I'd love to hear anything you'd like to say," I responded.

"Angela," she began, with tears filling her eyes, "I just wanted you to know how blessed my life has been. Jesus has given me so much. I am a rich woman because I know that He loves me. He has been good to me. I know it doesn't look like I have a lot, but I do. I am blessed, so very, very blessed."

I didn't quite know what to say. If any one of us had to trade places with her, we would surely call ourselves cursed. Without a home. Without a family. Without things or the means to provide for ourselves. People kill themselves because they fall into despair over losing everything and life becomes hopeless to them. This woman had every logical reason to lose hope, but instead she had chosen a kingdom heart. She was laying up treasure somewhere I couldn't see.

When a woman has a kingdom heart, she has an active understanding of what matters most to the heart of God. She energetically pursues Him with every piece of her being. She lives in the balance of passion and contentment. She learns to love well, give without regard to self, and forgive without hesitation.

The woman with a kingdom heart may have a duffel bag full of possessions or enough treasures to fill a mansion, but she has learned to hold them with an open hand.

With Open Hands

Not too long ago, I gave up almost everything I had. Before you think me holy, the choices weren't all mine, and being stripped down to nothing was possibly the most painful season of my life.

As I think back through those years, the degree of pain seemed to be multiplied because each of my fingers had to be pried, one by one, from the tight clutch I had wrapped around my treasures.

In my divorce, there was the stuff—you know, things you pack away in boxes, label with a permanent marker, and think you can't ever live without. And there were some relationships that got caught in the middle. And then there was my reputation. I didn't know how valuable it was to me until I heard the rumors and it was tarnished. And there were my dreams, each one falling to the ground as if a marksman had taken target practice with my longings. And soon after all those things were gone, my heart fell deeply into despair.

> *When you are holding everything with your hand open, then God is free to exchange His better for your good without so much pain in the transition.*

I cried over my lost treasure. My soul ached with a grief I had never known before. I knew that everything was gone, and for several months I just had to lie on my bed and tell myself to breathe. I was alive. I had my children and my family and my friends, but in a way it seemed as if I was dead without my treasures.

Hold everything with open hands. God began teaching me that in college. I thought I had understood Him, and I had for then, but not like this. I don't think we're ever allowed to grab hold of anything or anyone as though they matter more than the kingdom of heaven. When you are holding everything with your hand open, then God is free to exchange His better for your good without so much pain in the transition.

When you hold relationships with open hands, then people come in and out of your life as gifts of grace to be cherished and enjoyed, not objects to be owned and manipulated. When you hold your stuff with open hands, then plates break and washing machines leak and no one is too much worse for the wear. And then when you hold your dreams with open hands, you get to watch God resurrect what seemed dead and multiply what seemed small.

In these past years, I have learned that I don't ever want to hold on to anything that tightly again. It hurt like crazy to have it ripped from my aching hands. When you have lost all the things you called valuable on earth and wake up the next morning anyway, their importance becomes poignantly clear. I am coming to value things as blessings, gifts from the hand of God. And if they pass away again, so be it. What is more important is the treasure I am storing in heaven.

How do you hold on to your treasures? Do you clutch them tightly as if they are all you will ever have? Do you choke the life out of your relationships, believing that you have to remain in control? What if God wanted to improve your life or redirect your path and He needed your hands to be empty in order to take you there? Would He have to painfully pry your fingers, one by one, from the things you hold so tightly? Would He let you kick and scream and cry over your loss, so that He could pick you up and point you in the direction of kingdom treasure?

If you feel things slipping away, if you seem to have lost control, or if you instinctively want to grab hold of everything and pull it in tight, then maybe God is asking you to let go. Open your hands and let Him move His treasure in and out of your life. The blessing is that He always puts more into your open hands than you could have ever imagined there was room for.

Laying Up Treasures

Laying up treasure in heaven is about learning to value what is valuable to God. It will probably mean coming to appreciate the intangible riches of the kingdom inheritance more than the visible accumulation of stuff on earth. It might mean that your philosophy on wealth gets turned upside down by the teaching of Jesus, where mercy gets a better rating than mutual funds and sacrifice appraises higher than self. Laying up treasure will always be more about God's purpose and less about your personal accumulation. Kingdom values, the charac-

> *Laying up treasure in heaven is about learning to value what is valuable to God.*

teristics Jesus teaches in this sermon, are worth more in God's economy than all the rusting riches we have come to hold dear. I was an economics major in college, but the riches of God would never find their way onto any of the graphs I had to plot.

What do you think would be considered treasure in heaven? How about large accounts of forgiveness given? Drawers full of grace extended. A mattress stuffed with sacrifice and service and goodness. A cookie jar brimming with memories made and hugs given and tender looks across crowded rooms. A safe-deposit box packed with the secret life you have devoted to God. Maybe there is an old moving box stuffed with contentment. A scrapbook full of the joy you accumulated on the journey. And love—wouldn't it be great to need a garage out back just to hold all the love?

When I travel away for a weekend of ministry there are several ways to assign value to my time. My accountant might value my honorarium. The IRS values my taxes. The business folks value books sold. That's all fine, but none of it gets stored in heaven. What gets God's attention are lives changed. Treasure is stored in heaven when I value what God holds in esteem. Things like serving the church, sacrificing my time or my comfort for the needs of others, or crafting a message that meets a need within the body of Christ. Those acts of service are treasures to God.

As a mom, there are things that are very important to me on earth, but I am learning to sacrifice my desires in order to preserve the kingdom treasure in our family. I could be really intense about a clean house and orderly closets and neatly ironed shirts. I am predisposed toward organization. It's a firstborn thing. But I have realized that in this season, my desire for household perfection is really about my desire for appearance. I want to look like I have perfect kids and a perfect house. I don't. Every time I begin to value the appearance more than the children, I stress out our family. I forsake the kingdom treasure in order to have Barbie clothes organized by color and storybooks alphabetized by author. It's more important to God that I value the hearts of the children, that I teach them reasonable order, and that I learn to trade in the ironing for a game of Battleship every now and then.

When you and I begin to lay up treasure in heaven, it means that we are beginning to look more like the woman God had in mind. The things we acquire on earth are enjoyed with open hands, but the riches that motivate our hearts are the treasures that matter to God. People matter to God and hearts matter to God and love matters more than anything.

This Scripture says that your heart follows your treasure. Wouldn't it be amazing to be a woman whose treasure always leads her toward the kingdom?

The Stockpile

If we could inventory your treasure in heaven, what do you think we would find in your storeroom? If they handed us the key and we walked down a long corridor until we came to the door with your name, what would we discover inside? Would we open the door and run for cover when the contents came tumbling out? Or would we walk into an empty room with a dusty shoe box of belongings stashed over in the corner somewhere?

Understanding the value of a stockpile in heaven will shape your perspective and your actions on earth. When we have a treasure-in-heaven mind-set, pursuing bigger and better things on earth assumes its rightful place as ridiculous. There is a place called "good enough," and the people who store treasure in heaven know all about good enough. They wear nice clothes and drive a nice car and it's good enough. They can rest in the gracious provision of God. Their hands are open to His prompting to give things away. They stay in good enough hotels so that there is more to give. Their homes are good enough and they stop themselves from believing life will be empty unless they acquire bigger and better.

In a few days I'm going to visit those friends of mine who know a lot about kingdom wealth. I'll sleep on the pullout sofa or in one of the kids' rooms or wherever they have extra space. We'll stay up late and make peanut butter sandwiches for snacks. I'll probably meet four or five of their friends who just happen to stop by while I'm there. Everyone is welcome. The conversation is inclusive. The laughter is contagious. We'll tell the truth to one another and pray together and seek the heart of God. We won't spend a lot of money or do anything extravagant. And when it's time to leave, my heart will remind me, *I want to be rich like them.*

Questions for Reflection and Discussion

1. Which wealth strategy does your life seem to reflect: Accumulate Stuff or Stockpile in Heaven?

2. Would you say that you hold your things and your relationships with open hands or with tightly clenched fists? How has a tight fist caused you pain in the past?

3. Have you ever missed opportunities or a fresh direction from God because you would not open your hands and allow Him to take away and give more?

4. Does anyone in your life model for you a Stockpile-in-Heaven mentality? What do you find attractive about such an attitude or lifestyle?

5. How is God asking you to apply this instruction to your life? What would change or improve? How can you adjust your thinking so that you are more effectively storing up riches in heaven?

13

EXPECT A BRIDGE

⌒

*Therefore I tell you, do not worry about your life, what you will eat
or drink; or about your body, what you will wear. Is not life more
important than food, and the body more important than clothes?
(Matthew 6:25)*

*But seek first his kingdom and his righteousness, and all these
things will be given to you as well. (Matthew 6:33)*

ONCE UPON A TIME THERE WAS A WOMAN (THAT WOULD BE
me) who sometimes wished she was still a little girl (the me I used
to be). This little girl in the grown woman's body remembers
when she never worried about anything. She didn't worry about
being safe at night or what to make for dinner. She never gave one
thought to paying a bill or buying groceries or college funds. She
just skipped along, trusting the people who had always been trustworthy. Eventually, she met God and began to trust Him just the
same. That little girl had a cushy life and mushy love and a great,
big God that she never doubted.

Then one day the grown-up little girl realized that she was on a
journey and everyone else was on a journey too. We take a certain
path, and then we're forced to accept the consequences and surprises

that come to us on the way. Sometimes the road makes a quick turn we hadn't planned for. Sometimes there are accidents or mistakes and the journey is delayed. Sometimes we fall down and stay down and give up on ever completing the distance. And then sometimes attackers ambush our lives or pilfer our dreams or slip away into the night with our hearts.

On the journey, there are things that we need to survive and there are things that we desire to enjoy. And the grown-up little girl learned to worry about the things she thought she needed and the path that was in front of her and the would-be thieves hiding in the dark. The grown-up little girl came to believe that she was making this trip all alone. And she became so very afraid of the journey. She was afraid that her needs would not be met. And she was afraid that she'd never embrace her desires. And she was afraid that somebody or some awful thing would come along and take her life too soon. It seemed as though everyone she met on the journey was worried and filled with anxiety too.

Eventually, she heard about a place in the road up ahead. Evidently the path wasn't clear, and rumor had it that some of the road had washed away. She heard travelers murmuring that there was a bridge impossible to cross. Others had posted signs that read, "Turn Back, Road Closed, Bridge Out." And the grown-up little girl didn't know what to do. So she sat down to retrace her steps.

She knew that she belonged to God and this journey had been given to her by Him. He called this adventure a gift, and He promised to provide all she would need. When she looked back through the maps of her heart, she realized the great distance she had already come with God. He had overseen every step, provided every need, and carried every burden. In fact, she had never been alone for a minute. And she wondered why she had forgotten so easily and given herself over to fear.

But there was still the matter of the bridge up ahead. People said, *It can't be done. No one can figure it out. It won't be easy. It might cost too much. We don't have a plan. Maybe you should give up and stay here. Ever thought about turning around? It just might be too difficult to cross.* And the grown-up little girl looked back at the map of her past and ahead into the unknown and this is what she decided,

> *I don't know what God will do. I only know what He has already done. I can't see how we'll cross, but we're not there yet. Because I belong to God, I cannot embrace "impossible bridge" theology. I belong to the God who divided a sea to let His people through. I belong to the God who makes a new path through the desert. I belong to the God who built a bridge from heaven to earth just for me.*
>
> *I cannot see how to navigate what seems impossible, but I will keep walking. I do not know how all these needs will be met, but I will trust with each mile marker of His faithfulness that God will give greater provision than I can imagine.*
>
> *I will stand up and go forward and expect the bridge of His deliverance. A bridge of grace. An amazing superstructure of His glory where there seemed to be no way.*

So, when the grown-up little girl had retraced the steps of God's presence in her life and after she remembered that He had always provided, then she turned her heart in the direction of the kingdom and fixed her eyes on the Author and Perfecter of this faith journey. She gathered the ones she loved and held them close and whispered into their ears, "Not to worry. I don't know how I forgot, but we belong to God. This journey is His. We are going to walk toward the sound of His voice. And when the path seems impossible and the way is unclear, then we shall expect a bridge."

How Did I Forget?

A few years ago I was speaking at a women's conference in Florida. The local bookstore had come to be a part of the event, and they brought all kinds of things like stationery, mugs, and jewelry to sell. I don't usually bring things home for the children, but that weekend Taylor had really been on my mind. The bookstore had a little silver ring engraved with the words *Fear Not*. I thought it might be especially perfect for her. Our family was in the middle of divorce, and I hoped the reminder would give some comfort to her preteen heart.

When I got home and gave the present to Taylor, she loved the ring. But there was one problem—it was too small for her ring finger and too big for her pinky. We were both kind of bummed. It was a cool little ring with a powerful message. Taylor said, "Mom, see if it fits you." And amazingly, it fit my ring finger just right. So I began to wear the silver *Fear Not* ring.

In the next difficult months, I found myself tracing the outline of those words over and over. In the middle of the night, I'd lie awake and feel *Fear Not* like a blind woman learning to read Braille. I'd sit through meetings and find myself touching the words on the ring. I'd forget not to worry but then look at my finger and remember, "Breathe in, *Fear Not*. Breathe out, *Fear Not*." It became the message God used to carry me through those days.

You'd think that I wouldn't forget not to worry. It seems as though I should know better. I have studied these words about worry in the Sermon on the Mount a lot. I believe Jesus' instructions with all my heart. Through the years, this passage has given me such great comfort. But sometimes I act like a little girl and forget. Before I realize what's happened, my stomach hurts and my head aches and I can literally feel the worry.

I worry because I have four kids who keep outgrowing their jeans and I'm not sure how we'll buy new clothes. I worry when Taylor brags, "I'll be in high school next year," and all I can think about is the price of tuition for college. It seems like an impossible bridge. I worry when my friend needs more blood work because her enzymes came back abnormal.

I worry because I have known pain and I fear the pain again. I am afraid of being lost or rejected or unloved. I am afraid of being taken for a fool or being misunderstood or being used and tossed aside. I worry about what I cannot see and my lack of courage on really hard days. I am just a human being like you, and Jesus has to remind me not to worry about all these things.

One thought that gives me rest is knowing that Jesus is not mad about my worry. He doesn't want us to worry, but He obviously knew it came with our humanity. He told us not to worry because He realized our natural inclination toward anxiety. Jesus knows the intricacies of our humanness, our limitations, and our possibilities. He knows that even in our maturity, we need to be reminded of truths we have already learned. He knows that remembering runs out, and we long to hear of His love over and over again. He knows that weariness can set in, hearts can give up, and the spirit can become fretful and poor. So He said to us,

> Don't worry about your life.
> Don't worry about what you will eat or drink or wear.
> Don't worry about tomorrow.

Maybe you knew that already. Maybe you needed to be reminded too. What a tenderness He gives to us. He is not mad at our forgetfulness. He remembers our frailty and reminds us of a better way.

A few months ago, I stayed over at a friend's house. We had so much to catch up on and spent most of the evening sharing our life experiences, along with some of our anxieties and fears. We prayed and talked about Jesus and went to sleep that night encouraged that we both belonged to Him, trusting for every provision that we could not see.

The next morning I woke up with a very strong directive in my mind: "Give this friend your *Fear Not* ring." I walked into the kitchen in my pajamas and said, "I know this may sound kind of weird, but I think I am supposed to give you my *Fear Not* ring. It's a reminder for when you forget." She began to cry and then to sob. I told her it wasn't worth very much except I had cherished its message through the past year. And then for some reason I added, "I think you'll know when you're supposed to give it to the next person."

I just saw my friend last week and there on her right hand was my little silver ring with its powerful words, *Fear Not*. I smiled to myself, knowing it had come to mean as much to her as it had meant to me.

Do you need to hear that today? Just in case you forgot, I want to remind you, in the name of Jesus, *Fear Not*.

Seek First

I doubt that my mama remembers, but when I was in college she wrote a letter to me, promising that one day I'd be loved by a man. She said that obviously the man who could love me wasn't ready. God still had him in training. I remember her writing that "he is waiting in the wings, learning his lines, and will join you onstage at just the perfect time." And then she instructed me to give all my heart to the work God had put before me. At the end of the letter, she wrote Matthew 6:33:

> But seek first his kingdom
> and his righteousness,
> and all these things
> will be given to you as well.

That passage became my life verse; in many ways it is the banner God planted over my journey with Him. When I don't know what to do, I always fall back into these words: "Seek first his kingdom."

I love to think things through, process the options, weigh the evidence, and come up with short directives that seem logical and sane. The reason and logic of this phrase always bring me back to center, to all that really matters: *Seek first his kingdom*. It makes sense to me. It realigns my priorities. It reminds me to focus on what I may have forgotten. And then there is the amazing promise attached to this instruction: *And all these things will be given to you as well*.

> *When I don't know what to do, I always fall back into these words, "Seek first his kingdom."*

What things? All the things Jesus just talked to us about in verse 25. All the things you need to live. Whatever you will need for your body. Food. Clothes. Everything you will need for life, everything you and I might worry about, He promises to those who seek Him first.

The journey of following Jesus with our lives involves two dimensions: everything we can do plus His divinity. This verse comes with challenge and instruction: Focus your heart. Ask God what's next. Rearrange your priorities. Actively work with your hands or your mind for His glory. And then, at the end of everything you can do, expect God's divine provision for "all these things."

This verse has never failed me, and I expect that it will continue to direct every step I will take from here on into glory.

Reasons Not to Worry

Sometimes I get so spun around that I have to stop and remember why I am consciously choosing not to worry. Let's take a minute here to look at the reasons Jesus says the believer doesn't have to worry:

You are valuable. Jesus said that you are more valuable to God than the birds He always feeds and the lilies He always clothes. Have you forgotten that you are valuable to your Father in heaven?

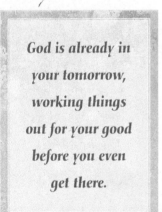

God is already in your tomorrow, working things out for your good before you even get there.

Have you forgotten that He calls you beautiful? Have you forgotten that He's wild about you? The world doesn't want you to believe it. Your family may never bring it up. But it's true, so very, very true. You are valuable to God, so He promised to provide "all these things" when you seek Him.

He knows what you need. Sometimes it might feel like God doesn't know what you need because you thought what you *wanted* was what you needed. This could possibly be a little too convicting for me at this moment. I am considering in my mind all the prayer requests I have put before God lately. I think I'll go back over those prayers with this one: "God, You know what I need even more than I do, so Your will be done in all these things. Amen."

He promises to give all that you need. God is a good Father. Not only does God know your needs, He is trustworthy to provide for them at the right time. I only have to look back on my life for just a minute to know that this is true.

He says there's enough trouble already. Worry adds trouble and fear, and we can all attest to the fact that there's already enough of that to go around. Jesus said, "Let tomorrow take care of itself and just look at Me today. Listen to My voice. Go where I lead." If you feel yourself wandering into the trouble of tomorrow, go back to Matthew 6:33 and let it reel you in. God is already in your tomorrow, working things out for your good before you even get there.

Watch God Provide

For twenty years, I have kept track of my financial budget on a yellow pad. On the left-hand side, I make a list of the monthly bills, and on the right-hand side there is a column for every month. One of my greatest joys in life is writing "PAID" in the square that corresponds to the bills for that month. When I get the bills paid, I stop for a minute on the way to the mailbox and touch every envelope and thank God for the means to pay them. I don't ever want to forget where each penny comes from. I walk in such great financial dependence on God's provision that I am keenly aware of His gifts.

This last year I sat down to draw a new budget page on my yellow pad. At the top of the paper I wrote: "Watch God provide, again!" I have to tell you that when I wrote those words, I didn't know how He was going to do it. I saw all those little squares and it felt overwhelming to me. This month is October and I paid my bills yesterday. I sat at the kitchen table with tears in my eyes, looking at every square that had been marked paid for this year. I am so very grateful.

You know, this journey is a tough one. We could find a lot to worry about. We could make up things to get sick over. We could say to one another, "What will we do in two years, or four years, or ten?"

Jesus said that it's beautiful to Him when we stop doing that. He is saying to us,

As you go, as you make this incredible journey called life, and you get to a place where the road seems to end, then expect the God who loves you to build a bridge that will take you across.

I come from a long line of worriers. I could be good at it if I tried. I've had training. I could even become prideful about the great lengths I could go to in order to worry more. But I am choosing God instead.

I am the little girl in the grown-up woman's body who is not making this journey alone. It is only when my heart is downcast and I have turned my eyes away from the kingdom that I believe I am by myself. I have heard the strong voice of Jesus reminding me to seek Him first. More and more I am remembering who I belong to. Less and less I am listening to the fears of others.

I am going forward even when I cannot see. My worries are becoming trampled underneath the feet of my obedience. I sense the pleasure God takes in this offering.

Maybe the road is washed out ahead. Maybe others have turned around and given up. But I belong to Jesus and I will confidently expect a bridge.

May you trust Him for your bridge too.

Questions for Reflection and Discussion

1. As you look ahead into your journey, where do you fear that a bridge is out or that you won't find a way? What are the rumors that make you afraid?

2. Now look back at your journey with God. How has He been faithful? How has He provided when you didn't believe there was a way?

3. Matthew 6:33 is my life verse. Do you have a life verse? A Scripture that has given guidance like a banner across your path?

4. Do you forget that you belong to God? Do you forget that over and over He says to us, "Fear not"? Where is God shouting "Fear not" to you right now?

5. Where do you need to say to God, "I am walking forward by faith. I belong to You, and I will expect that You will provide a bridge over what seems impossible"?

14

LAY IT DOWN

⌒

Do not judge, or you too will be judged. (Matthew 7:1)

*Why do you look at the speck of sawdust in your brother's eye and
pay no attention to the plank in your own eye? How can you say to
your brother, "Let me take the speck out of your eye," when all the
time there is a plank in your own eye? You hypocrite, first take the
plank out of your own eye, and then you will see clearly to remove
the speck from your brother's eye. (Matthew 7:3–5)*

*So in everything, do to others what you would have them do to
you. (Matthew 7:12)*

*I care very little if I am judged by you or by any human court;
indeed, I do not even judge myself. My conscience is clear, but that
does not make me innocent. It is the Lord who judges me. Therefore
judge nothing before the appointed time; wait till the Lord comes.
He will bring to light what is hidden in darkness and will expose
the motives of men's hearts. (1 Corinthians 4:3–5)*

THERE IS A LITTLE WOODEN SIGN THAT HANGS BESIDE THE
door in my kitchen. It reads, *Thou Shall Not Tattle.* I bought it for

the children a few years ago, but I have decided it's time to hang a few more instructions underneath it. Things like:

- Thou shall not walk into a room and immediately groan with displeasure.
- Thou shall not laugh at the knots in your brother's shoestrings.
- Thou shall not use tones that give others the impression you will surely die if forced to say something nice.
- Thou shall not assume that everyone else in the family is bad and conspired to ruin the backpack that you yourself left outside, overnight, in the driveway.
- Thou shall not judge your younger siblings' ability to spell a word that you could not spell until this year.
- Thou shall not roam to and fro throughout the house, looking for something negative to say, someone to hold in a headlock, or rubber bands to pop across the room.
- Thou shall not come into my presence unless you're happy, with a smile on your face and something pleasant to say. (That one may be a little strong.)

I have decided that left to our natural inclination, we drift toward negativity. I see it in my own children. I daily find myself correcting their tones and their tendency to judge one another quickly. And I can see the same predisposition in my own heart.

When I am tired or inconvenienced or treated unfairly, my mind can wander toward condemnation. I was on a field trip to the zoo with AnnaGrace a few days ago and it was cold. I had on a turtleneck sweater, sweatshirt, and overcoat and I was still miserable. A few hours into you've-seen-one-elephant-you've-seen-them-all and trying to locate sleeping tigers behind rocks, I could feel my spirit sinking and my negativity rising. I was frozen and realized that I possessed definite whiny-baby potential. There was judgment inside of me that wanted to get out. I started asking myself what teacher thought it was a good idea to go to the zoo and eat lunch outside with the animals? Didn't they know that it could be cold and I'd be grumpy and I'd have to fake it as though I loved it the whole time? I thought about saying something about being frozen a few times, but finally decided to buy a hot chocolate and keep quiet. I was frustrated about being inconveniently cold, but I was even more disappointed with my heart's quick inclination toward judgment.

So tell me, is there any good that happens when we allow ourselves to become judgmental or come through the door with a negative spirit? I've never seen one heart mended in judgment. No one is encouraged or built up. No one is motivated to change because he or she was the recipient of sustained cynicism, condemnation, or painful words. Why is it so much easier to find fault? Why do people spend huge amounts of energy and emotion being negative? What if they just tried one time to see things differently? Decided to bite their tongues instead of speaking recklessly? Worked on getting the planks out of their own eyes first?

This may end up being my soapbox chapter, so you might want to skip this one if you're not ready for it. I can already feel myself getting wired about this. Maybe it's because I see the drift toward judgment in my preteen and teenage children. Maybe it's because I feel my own heart become jaded at times. Maybe it's because I just read my e-mail.

The Sting of Judgment

I get a lot of great e-mails. Cool stories about what God is doing in the lives and hearts of women all over the world. Sometimes very heart-wrenching accounts of woundedness, brokenness, or rejection. Sometimes stories of great spiritual victories. But then, every once in a while, there is a nasty letter sent to me from someone who claims to love Jesus. These are the people who have chosen for themselves the ministry of discouragement. I just happened to read a yucky letter this morning that someone had posted about me on another Web site.

A woman I haven't met was mad that I did not say in my last book that I am divorced. She was so mad that she sat down and took the time to find an outlet for her anger on the Internet. When I stumbled across her intense words, I could feel my heart breaking all over again. Hot tears began to sting my eyes, and then there was the knot that found its way into my throat. I stared at my computer and felt so misunderstood by someone who didn't take the time to write to me personally. She could have condemned me in private before she posted on the Web. I felt pounded unfairly. I felt incredibly judged without even so much as a trial.

If I could find her, I'd tell her that I wasn't divorced when I turned in the book. I had no idea what was going to happen in my marriage at the time. I'd tell her that my church knew everything. My publisher walked with me. We made the best decisions we could with everything that was in front of us. A part of me wants to call her up and tell her enough to calm her down, but I can't. I guess I am most sad in knowing that even if I could find her and speak to her, it probably wouldn't help. I imagine that she'd still find a reason to judge.

When someone wants to find something wrong, it comes easy for that person. So many of us are great speck detectors. We are quick to see what's wrong, imagine something covert, or fabricate criticism. Sometimes I just want to scream, "Get a life; I mean a real life, with something to do that matters in this world. Be vulnerable and real and tell the truth and see how it feels to be recklessly judged by someone you've never met." I guess I probably shouldn't say that. Maybe I'll find kinder words for that lady. Maybe I'll pray for her. Condemnation hurts a lot. It seems as though just about the time we get over the last heartache, someone else from the body of Christ comes along and makes it hurt again. Ever heard of shooting your wounded? We do that sometimes.

Can you tell I'm sad and kind of mad? Misinformed, reckless judgment ought to get us riled up. It serves no purpose in the kingdom of heaven. We have so much more to do with our lives. Jesus said not to judge. It tarnishes the beautiful offering.

We Don't Have Permission

Dallas Willard writes, "We must beware of believing that it is okay for us to condemn as long as we are condemning the right things. It is not so simple as all that. I can trust Jesus to go into the temple and drive out those who were profiting from religion, beating them with a rope. I cannot trust myself to do so."

In this beautiful-life discourse, Jesus has given us so many gracious instructions. Sometimes He has asked us to put on a kingdom attitude that bears His likeness. Other times, He directs us to choose attributes and actions that reflect the heart of the Father. But here, Jesus uses strong language to require us to lay something down. He wants us to lay down our judgment, our critical spirit, our negativity, our cynicism, and our disapproval. He wants us to give it up today—permanently.

> *The life God wants for you and me doesn't contain even a hint of judgment.*

The life God wants for you and me doesn't contain even a hint of judgment. He isn't talking about discernment or wisdom in regard to judging circumstances. This instruction is a lesson on condemnation. Jesus never gives us permission to condemn others. He doesn't mince words when He says,

> Do not judge, or you too will be judged. For in the same way you judge others, you will be judged, and with the measure you use, it will be measured to you. (Matthew 7:1–2)

> You hypocrite, first take the plank out of your own eye, and then you will see clearly to remove the speck from your brother's eye. (Matthew 7:5)

Jesus calls the one inclined to condemnation a hypocrite. The hypocrite is easy to spot in this context because the condemning spirit always gives her away. The mere fact that we have become judgmental is the first clue that we do not have the kingdom heart Jesus has been talking about in this passage. The judgmental spirit has companions in anger, contempt, and self-righteousness. The woman who is quick to judge finds herself blind to the humanity and heart of other people. She is so blinded by the plank of her judgment that she cannot see how to help others with the specks of their sins.

> *The woman who is quick to judge finds herself blind to the humanity and heart of the other person.*

181

I Have Been Stupid

I certainly have been judged, but so much worse, I have been judgmental. I have heard condemning thoughts ricochet through my head, and then I have said things out loud that I regret. Maybe the two most prominent areas where I have been quietly judgmental are in the regard to blatant sin and the practice of faith. I can't tell you how relieved I am that God is radically transforming my stupid heart. I truly mean it. I was stupid and, part of the time, I was ignorant. Sometimes when you look back at where you have been it's embarrassing. I am so very ashamed of my narrow-minded past.

Thankfully, God loved me enough not to leave me stupid. He sent two powerful forces to begin to transform my heart . . . a friend and a church.

I have written about my friend Carlye before. Her son, Rob, died from the complications of drug and alcohol addiction. Their amazing family fought and cried their way through eighteen very long years, trying to save his life. They have all experienced such incredible pain, grief, and heartache. But that's not the only battle Carlye has known. She has given me permission to tell you that before she was a believer she became pregnant and was eventually pressured into an illegal abortion. After that, there was a difficult first marriage to Rob's dad that ended in divorce.

Today, Carlye has been married to Jerry for thirty-six years. They have a great son named Dace, and they are all devoted followers of Christ. Carlye volunteers at a local pregnancy center where she counsels young women who are considering abortion, many of them addicts, all of them afraid. Almost every week, she tells me about another woman who prayed to receive Christ as her Savior. God is using Carlye and her testimony in such a powerful way. I believe that women come to Christ after they have spent time with her because maybe for the first time in their lives, because of her vulnerability, brokenness, and godliness, they have felt no condemnation.

Choices and consequences and devastation have taken the judgment from Carlye's spirit. When you are with her, you know that you are accepted. When we've talked about it, she says, "Angela, you never know where people have been, what they've been through, or why they made a decision you would disagree with. You can't judge them. Leave that to God and love them instead." It would be one thing if she only had words, but my amazing friend truly lives and loves without condemnation.

I know for certain that God sent Carlye into my life because He didn't want to leave me stupid. I had been quick to judge in regard to blatant sin, quick to assign a label to people and then find a way to detach from them and move away. But God wanted me to meet and fall in love with a woman who would model for me no condemnation. He wanted me to be transformed by her open heart and her open mind and the loving mercy and grace she extends to everyone she meets. God has given us a beautiful friendship. We are almost at twenty years of her gentle shaping in my life. What's so cool is that she loved me from the very beginning when I was an arrogant, smart seminary student. And she loves me now, broken and still in process.

There is still the other area where I have been judgmental. I have judged others in regard to the practice of faith. I was raised as an evangelical, trained by some of the finest Bible and theology professors in the world, and discipled in wonderful churches. I am so grateful for the great men and women who have guided my education and ministry. I would not choose one path or one person differently.

But somewhere along the way, I began to draw a box around my faith. A very tight box where I kept God and my brilliant Bible answers and the way we worship. I lived and judged from inside those thick walls of arrogance. And honestly, here's what's creepy,

I thought that I was absolutely right and everyone outside the box was absolutely wrong.

Then God plopped me into an evangelical church with some folks who are charismatic. I have come to respect and love people who worship differently than I do. They interpret a few passages of Scripture differently and sometimes pray in ways I'd never known before. I have found that some of the most godly, pure in spirit, faithful, and compassionate men and women are outside my box, and I could have missed them if God had left me stupid. I have come to realize that God is outside my box, guiding and blessing those folks too.

He has stretched me like crazy. I'm so sorry that it has taken me a long time to get it. Sometimes fear breeds judgment, and God is taking away my fears. Sometimes ignorance leads us into condemnation. God is now giving me understanding and grace.

The other day, I was at the Rescue Mission. A woman asked if she could pray for me. I told her I'd love that. I was sitting and she began to pray over me. She danced around me and cried for me and spoke in tongues and physically stretched herself over me and petitioned Jesus for His anointing and blessing in my life. This praying woman was outside my box, way outside the realm of where I have allowed myself to be comfortable in the past. Five years ago I would have missed her heart because of the plank of my judgment. Ten years ago I would have felt afraid because I was so smart and legalistic. A few days ago, I fell in love with that praying lady.

I was peaceful on the inside as she prayed. I did not feel anxious or judgmental. I loved that her prayers were different from anything I've ever known. I loved that we were praying to the same Father through the same Holy Spirit in the name of the same Jesus. As we were leaving, one of my friends said, "I've never seen any praying like that." I said, "Me neither, but I'll take it. All day long, I'll take it."

Jesus is removing my stupid heart of judgment and condemnation, and I am so grateful to lay it all down for His glory.

The Way Out

I guess that divorce is one of the worst things that ever happened to me. But the brokenness has transformed my heart like nothing else could. On this side of that kind of pain, I can see a little more clearly. People don't want messy lives and torn-up marriages and addicted kids. They don't want to be bound to sin. They are ashamed of their awful mistakes. You don't really have to beat them up anymore. They can spend a lifetime berating themselves. So instead of more contempt and disgrace, what if we offered them a way out?

What if we came alongside their pain and took them by the hand into the presence of God? What if we stayed with them until they had been truly introduced to the only One who can forgive and heal and restore? What if we weren't afraid of their pasts? What if we could see the God of their future? What if the people who come into our lives felt no condemnation? Can you imagine their relief? Can you imagine how it might feel to step from the shadows of shame and into the bright love of God's forgiveness and grace? Did you know that God wants you to lead them out? He wants you to lay down your judgment so that His merciful love can work through you.

About three or four times in the past few years, I have had to do something in direct opposition to my personality. I have had to speak with someone who wanted more answers than I could give. When our conversation was over, I knew each person was not satisfied, and I had to walk away realizing that I was still the object of each one's judgment. The pleaser in me wants to make everybody happy. I want to find the e-mail woman and take her to lunch and work it all out. But here is the truth from God's Word. This is where the givers and the receivers of judgment can find their way out:

Therefore, there is now no condemnation for those who are in Christ Jesus. (Romans 8:1)

When you and I enter into a relationship with Jesus Christ, there is a new reality that runs counter to our natural inclination. Because of Jesus, condemnation is now irrelevant. Not only does Jesus not condemn you, but also because of His love, He died for you and intervenes at the right hand of the Father in heaven on your behalf. You and I are covered by His declaration that because we belong to Him, we are no longer condemned.

Paul goes on to say in that same chapter in Romans,

> Nothing can separate us from the love of God that is in Jesus Christ our Lord. (Verses 8:33–35)

Nothing can separate you from the One who does not condemn. We don't have to play these negative games anymore. We don't have to find fault or assign guilt or heap shame. Don't you think it's time to lay it down? Don't you think it would be a sweet offering to give not and receive not?

If I could hang a big wooden sign beside my door to remind me to act beautifully, maybe it would say,

> Guess what? God is outside the box of your understanding.
> You are not condemned and neither are they.
> Now lay it down and let somebody know what no condemnation
>   feels like.
> By the way, that would be a great way to show them Jesus.

I think I should lay it down and post a letter to the lady who's angry with me. "Its okay," I'll tell her. "I'm not mad at you and Jesus is not mad at either one of us."

Questions for Reflection and Discussion

1. Do you have a natural inclination toward negativity or judgment? How is God speaking to you through the words of Jesus in regard to your attitude?

2. Did you realize that the plank of your judgment can keep you from helping others with the speck of their sin? Can you imagine what it would feel like to just lay down your judgment and begin to love others as freely as Jesus does?

3. Did you realize that those who are quick to judge just highlight for everyone the depth of their spiritual immaturity? How would you rate your spiritual maturity in regard to this area?

4. There are so many around us who need a way out more than they need our continued judgment. Is there someone in your life who needs to know that "there is now no condemnation"? No condemnation from Jesus and no condemnation from you.

5. What kind of sign would you hang beside your door to remind you to act beautifully?

15

TAKE THE NARROW GATE

‿

Enter through the narrow gate. For wide is the gate and broad is the road that leads to destruction, and many enter through it. But small is the gate and narrow the road that leads to life, and only a few find it. (Matthew 7:13–14)

EVERY DAY, SOMETIMES SEVERAL TIMES A DAY, I MAKE THE drive back and forth to my kids' school. It's a twenty-minute trip one way, and just a mile away from the school, we make a left turn onto the most direct route. It's a very narrow, winding road without guardrails. At one point the road hangs over the side of what feels like a small Tennessee mountain. It's a dangerous road, and nobody likes it. Up until last year, it was only wide enough for one car. So if you met another car coming or going, someone had to back up and let the other car pass. The state worked on the road for a few days and now two cars can pass, but only very slowly, making sure that side-view mirrors do not collide.

Every time I turn onto that road, I think about dying. I'm not kidding. I have visions of my car slipping over the side of the mountain because I have edged over too far to let another car pass. I imagine that a few days will go by and my kids will still be sitting at school, and they'll wonder where Mom is. Then one of them will offer, "I bet she died on the scary road."

As bad as it is by day, that road is a million times worse at night. No streetlights. Lots of winding and turning. You're unable to see around the next curve and you have that ever-present feeling that you're going over the side. Spooky. My kids hate the scary road. I hate it too. Except it's the most direct way to school.

We could make the journey several other ways. None of the other roads to school involve mountains. They all have painted lines and enough room to drive normally. But all the other routes add about ten minutes to the drive. So we keep taking the narrow road.

There is something about our experience with narrow roads that makes us afraid of Jesus' words in this passage. It feels scary to some and unpleasant to others. Some people follow God, but they have turned the narrow path into a list of rigid rules. Others follow God, but they have trouble with His instruction, so they try to walk the widest narrow path possible.

Mad About the Narrow Road

I have a friend who ponders God with great devotion. She reads feverishly and always wants to discuss her new insights into God's character. All of her growing-up life, she has been consumed with the idea that we have to live a life that is pleasing to God out of duty. And all of her life she felt that she came up short. She wants to offer a beautiful life back to God, but she thinks that nothing she can give is good enough.

She thinks that God is mad at her. She believes that when she sins, He turns His back on her. She feels as if He must be a cosmic state trooper who writes wide-path citations, continues to tabulate bad points for her record, and can't wait to catch her sinning enough that He can finally take away her license to enjoy life.

We have talked and talked and talked about the net of grace. She says, "I hear you," but she can't find any rest. She has this notion that God requires a perfect offering. I say, "Well, He did require a perfect offering. That was Jesus. Now, because of Jesus, we can come to God, in our imperfection, and be received as beautiful." My friend needs to surrender. I've told her at least fourteen million times. She knows it. And one day, she'll finally give up and fall back into the net of God's acceptance. But until then, she's driving us both crazy.

My friend has swung from both sides of the pendulum. For years, she kept the rules and that didn't work, and then sometime after college, she broke all the rules and felt awful. The narrow path makes her mad and the wide path destroys her life. I knew she was going to be huffy when I told her about this chapter, and she was. She wants to skip this narrow-road part. I know some other people who want to skip this part too.

People don't like thinking that the life God blesses is through a narrow gate, down a narrow path. That feels like the spooky road to them. Most of us want the interstate life with lots of room to weave in and out, a variety of exits and options, and never any citations for driving recklessly. Most of us just want to live any way we please. We'd like to apply all the grace verses and disregard all the narrow-road verses. Thankfully, with God, both come wrapped in the same package. The call toward the narrow gate is given inside the gracious embrace of God's love and protection.

No Other Way

We are almost at the end of Jesus' sermon to His followers that day. With these words about the narrow gate, He is beginning to wrap it up. He has just given a body of instruction that will guide the lives of believers for all generations to come. And with these last words, Jesus is preparing to send His listeners out to live a life that He calls beautiful and blessed.

What did He mean in these verses? What is the application for us? Let's walk slowly here and make sure we understand His direction and His heart. In verse 13, Jesus said,

Enter through the narrow gate.

The narrow gate that He is referring to is the way to salvation. In John 10:9, He goes on to say,

I am the gate; whoever enters through me will be saved.

And then in John 14:6,

I am the way and the truth and the life. No one comes to the Father except through me.

The narrow gate is Jesus Himself, the holy and perfect Son of our living God. He is the only way to be saved, and He is the only entrance into eternity. Every other way leads to destruction and death. Every other gate is a dead end.

After a conference a few weeks ago, a woman came rushing out to meet me. She was young and interesting-looking with lots of piercings and tattoos. She said, "I just wanted to tell you that I really enjoyed everything you had to say. I also wanted you to know that I am a practicing witch who is very committed to my god. My aunt made me come today, but I felt my god present with your God."

I felt such great compassion for her misunderstanding. I could see in her eyes the desire to be right but heard in her words that she was incredibly wrong. I firmly but gently told her that there is only one

AS YOU GO

true God. She adamantly disagreed. I promised that I would pray for her to be able to hear His voice above any other voice in her head. She said that she would never recant her faith or her practice, but thought we could both be on the path together. I reminded her of these verses about the narrow gate. There is only one way, no variations, no other gods, no options. We parted that day with a hug, in firm disagreement on the way that leads to life and eternity. My heart aches for her. And I continue to pray for her understanding.

Jesus said that many will choose the wide gate that leads to destruction. The wide gate is any other way except Jesus. He is the narrow gate, and, apart from Him, there is no way to be saved.

The Narrow Road

On the other side of the narrow gate is the narrow road. This is where some of us feel antsy, or even like my girlfriend, mad. Maybe it's because the narrow path has been misinterpreted or misrepresented. Here is what the narrow road is not:

- The narrow road is not narrow-mindedness.
- The narrow road is not a list of rules to be kept.
- The narrow road is not doctrinal correctness.
- The narrow road is not a lonely road.
- The narrow road is not fraught with haughtiness, television evangelists, and street-corner, Bible-thumping screamers.
- The narrow road is not a miserable "I guess I'll have to be a missionary in the jungle" life.
- The narrow road is not the opposite of everything good and fun and desirable.

Jesus said in John 14:23,

If anyone loves me, he will obey my teaching.

The narrow road is obedience. The narrow road is a woman deciding to live her life as a beautiful offering to God. The narrow road turns a woman in the direction of her Father and sends her on the journey toward His likeness. Jesus said,

Narrow [is] the road that leads to life, and only a few find it. (Matthew 7:14)

Jesus spent a whole sermon talking about the kingdom life. The life He desires for you on this earth. A life that is blessed. The life that reflects the heart and mind of the Father. He says that, apart from obedience, we will not know this kingdom life that He offers to us so freely. The opposite of the narrow road is simply choosing to live however you please.

However You Please

I think that a lot of the people I know would like to enter through the narrow gate and then take the wide road. They believe that Jesus is the only way to be saved and they want that, but they'd prefer to avoid all His living instructions and make the rest of their journey on a superhighway. There are believers who know better and still choose to take the wide road. They live however they please with a few church services thrown in for good measure.

All my Christian friends who are taking the wide path are miserable. I mean it. They can't figure out what in the world is wrong. They have been called to the narrow path, but want the wide path and its seeming enticements. They spend hours in therapy trying to reconcile the crazy roads they're taking. They are frustrated with God for not coming through . . . again, on the wide road. And they're wasting a whole lot of years in flat-out disobedience, wrecking their hearts and their calling.

There is such a conflict going on in their souls. The Holy Spirit has taken up residence, and His job is to give step-by-step direction for living. We take the narrow path every time we choose to respond to the Holy Spirit in obedience. The wide path keeps us in opposition to His leading. It's painful to watch my friends struggle with this truth. They believe that they deserve to be free, and it's out there somewhere beyond the guardrails of God's protection.

> We take the narrow path every time we choose to respond to the Holy Spirit in obedience.

Jesus said that you can't live however you please and enjoy His kingdom blessings. I think that makes some people mad. And they'll probably be even madder when I tell them that the wide road is a mark of spiritual immaturity. Kicking and screaming to live however you please is the sign of a baby Christian. A small faith. Lack of understanding.

We talked about God's economy earlier. Sometimes it just doesn't make sense to us, so we try to figure out another way. We want to be free, so we run away from God. We choose all the things that keep us on the wide path and then one day we wake up and realize that we are in bondage, prisoners to our disobedience. But when we choose the narrow gate and the narrow road and hide ourselves in the shelter of His strong embrace, then we are finally free. I know it's hard to get your head around. But it's true. We desire the freedom that Jesus says comes from obedience. But we don't believe that the freedom could really be born of obedience, so we run toward bondage and hope there is an alternate route.

Now that will make you crazy.

Free to Obey

In writing every one of these pages, I have prayed for you. I have prayed that you will desire to live your life as a beautiful love-offering to God. I have prayed that you will understand that God knows the limitations of your humanity and He's not mad at you about it. Right now I am praying that you will know God wants your obedience, but He does not expect your perfection. Remember? He knows it's just you. He remembers that you need a Savior. He has made a way. There is a net of grace.

We give up on obedience when we misunderstand it as a demand for perfection. To be obedient to the instruction of Jesus is a gift back to God. You and I are free to obey, and God has made it easy for us.

I want to make this as simple as possible, so please forgive me if I oversimplify or insult your intelligence. I don't mean to.

God loves you so much.
He made a way through Jesus to save you for eternity.
In the Sermon on the Mount, Jesus gives us living instructions.
God promises to bless that life. He calls it the kingdom life.
The only way to live the kingdom life is through obedience
　　to the instructions.
Obedience is the narrow road.
The road leads to God and becoming more like God.

Obedience means that you keep walking toward God. No
matter what.
All you have to do is keep looking at God.
In your weakness, look for God.
In your failure, find His gaze.
In your imperfection, keep turning in His direction.
You will stay on the narrow path when you have set your eyes
on God.

I believe that if you can understand that obedience is not perfection then you might begin to think, *I can do that. I can hang in
there.* If we are on a path, then the goal is to keep moving in the
direction of God. Some days we will be sprinting. Some days
standing still. Some days lying flat on our faces. But maybe what
matters more than anything—sprinting, standing, or fallen—is that
we keep our eyes firmly fixed on the One who calls us by name.
The One who calls us beautiful. The One who comes to carry us.
The One who covers our lack with His grace.

To obey means that you believe God's ways are right. To obey
reflects your heart of confidence in His sovereignty. To obey is to
rest in His authority as Creator, Redeemer, and Keeper.

Kingdom obedience becomes kingdom abundance.

Kingdom Abundance

I have never regretted obeying Jesus. Not one time. Never. I have
thought it was going to be awful. I have feared the outcome of
truth-telling and going against the popular vote. But to this day, I
have never regretted when I have responded to God in obedience.

Remember the Beatitudes that we called the When You Are's?
Did you hear Jesus saying over and over that He is waiting to bless

your life? Even in your weakness and humanity, He (God) desires to pour His abundance over your obedience. Even when you are broken, even when you don't think you are enough, even when you are persecuted, even then, your obedience brings His blessing.

Kingdom abundance means that you have full access to heaven, a hearing with God in a moment's prayer, divine protection, guidance, and the lavish riches of forgiveness, grace, peace, and mercy. When there is abundance, there is more than you need. Enough to give away. Enough for tomorrow. Enough for eternity.

> *Even in your weakness and humanity, He (God) desires to pour His abundance over your obedience.*

When you and I decide to obey, we have decided to trust that God knows more. Would you humble your heart and choose the narrow gate, follow the narrow road of obedience, and trust that waiting for you is the kingdom abundance of God's blessing?

⌒

My friend who has taken the wide path is missing the blessing. She sits with her counselor week after week and wonders why life seems so empty. She lacks discernment in her judgment. She comes up against the consequences of disobedience and blames God. She is mad about the way life turns out when she has chosen to blatantly disregard God's instruction. I love my friend so much. I ache over her pain. I tell her all the time, "Try the narrow path. There is a freedom there that you've never known." I keep believing that one day she'll get there. One day she'll stop insisting on her own way and trust God and His narrow way.

The narrow road is not the scary road. It is a trusted path—the one Jesus Himself walked down. It's the most direct road to God. The safest path into His arms. The avenue of His abundance.

Questions for Reflection and Discussion

1. Where would you say that you are living these days? Narrow road or wide interstate?

2. What are some other misconceptions of the narrow road? Why do so many of us want to avoid it?

3. Why does God say that you can't just live however you please?

4. How can the abundant live come to the woman on the narrow path? Won't it always feel as if you are missing out? Sacrificing pleasure?

5. What is God doing in regard to your thoughts about obedience? Do you feel yourself desiring a life of obedience?

16

BUILD ON THE ROCK

~

Everyone who hears these words of mine and puts them into practice is like a wise man who built his house on the rock. The rain came down, the streams rose, and the winds blew and beat against that house; yet it did not fall, because it had its foundation on the rock. (Matthew 7:24–25)

But everyone who hears these words of mine and does not put them into practice is like a foolish man who built his house on sand. (Matthew 7:26)

WHEN I AM PREPARING A NEW TALK FOR A GROUP OF women, I will choose a theme, the central passages, and the stories that tie it all together. At the end of my preparation, I will always ask myself, "What does it matter?" Sometimes I will even write at the bottom of my page, "So what?" to remind myself that whatever we're studying has to matter to God and each woman has to be able to see how it matters for her life.

We are at the end of Jesus' teaching in the Sermon on the Mount. These last verses about building on the rock instead of the sand give us His final instruction, the summary of His sermon, and the reason it all matters.

Jesus said that when we begin to work His sermon into our

lives, it's like building a house on solid rock. It will stand firm against every trial and storm that comes against it. But to live apart from His words is like building a house on sinking sand.

⌒

My dear sister in Christ. My friend. Fellow journeywoman. Feminine soul. I believe that we can return God's love to us with our lives. I think that we can bless Him with an offering that He calls beautiful. I believe that we can decide to turn our lives in the direction of God and stay faithful to look toward Him until we see Him face-to-face. I believe that no matter where you have been or how much trouble you have known, your life can become a strong house built on the solid foundation of Jesus Christ.

God is not mad at us or out to get us. I think He means it when He says that He casts our sin as far as the east is from the west and remembers it no more. I believe with all my heart that He is wild for you and for me. I think that we have become hesitant in our lives and fearful to move toward Him because we have not really known the depth of His love and desire for us.

This sermon matters because these are the words of Jesus. He has given these life teachings to us so that we will know the characteristics of a beautiful offering. In this last As You Go instruction, Jesus is saying to us,

As you go, take everything that I have just given to you and build an amazing life to the glory of God.

An Amazing Life

How many women do you know with an amazing life, built and lived for the glory of God? I know some, but not enough. Jesus has made a way for each of us to build on the Rock and live for His renown. I want to live an amazing life! I hope it's your desire as well.

I want to know what it means to find my breath and being in the person of Jesus Christ. I want to see what life would turn out like if every single morning I woke up and dedicated my heart and minutes to the purposes of God. I want to know what children turn out like when their mom lives her live surrendered to Jesus. I wonder what God can do with a woman who is empty and broken and fully His.

In this passage, Jesus says that we begin to be that kind of a woman when we decide to do more than listen and ponder. We become women with amazing lives when we begin to put Jesus' words into practice.

> *We become women with amazing lives when we begin to put Jesus' words into practice.*

One Bite at a Time

How do you eat an elephant? One little bite at a time. Beginning to put on the words of Jesus may feel like an elephant to you. It can to me. Sometimes I am overwhelmed by all the change that needs to happen in my life. Sometimes I am fatigued by the endlessness of the journey. Sometimes I think that I just can't become amazing because I'm not strong enough or brave enough.

Because of my schedule and the schedules of the children, I live by one cardinal rule . . . Do what's next. I will have a meltdown if I try to work on a project that's two weeks out. All I can do is what's required next. The width of my reach may broaden when the children are older, but for now, I have calendars everywhere, field trip schedules posted, and my schedule outlined beside theirs with spelling tests and book deadlines thrown in for extra stress. All I can do is take the next step. Pack the next lunch. Fold another load of clothes. Do the next thing, however small it may seem.

I want to have a great big understanding of Jesus and His Word. I want to know the Bible and take it into my life. But some days I have to approach my spiritual life like it's an elephant. I give myself grace when all I can do is take the small bite. Do the next thing. Read one chapter that I ponder through the day. Write a few words in my journal that give insight to my heart. Respond to an injustice more like Jesus and less like me. Try to be faithful, even in small ways, even though I wish I could tackle it all at once.

Jesus said that we are supposed to build our house on the rock. The rock that He is referring to is Himself. We are supposed to build our lives on the solid foundation of Jesus. Maybe you have already begun. Maybe you have been delayed. Maybe it seems like an elephant that you can't tackle. But is there one small step you can take? One small bite that will get you started?

In our relationship with Jesus, all He requires is that we do the next thing. The next thing for you may mean getting yourself back into His presence and then learning to stay there consistently. It may mean praying about a specific weakness and then responding when God gives direction. It might mean stepping into an unknown or taking a risk or stretching yourself in ways you had not anticipated. However small the step, it is a step in the direction of Jesus and His likeness.

The amazing life, the beautiful offering, the life God dreamed of for you and me begins on the solid foundation of Jesus Christ. I imagine some of you have already known the sinking sand of many other beginnings. It's okay. Tear it all down and start over right.

Come back to the only sure footing. We get to start over with God. We get second chances and new beginnings and renewed dreams. It is never too late to build an amazing life with Christ. You are never too old to get a new foundation and a fresh start.

So this very day, what can you do—big or small—to begin building your life on the Rock?

The House of Character

Just exactly what does Jesus want us to build? He wants us to build a house of strong character. Do you remember Jesus' words toward the end of the book of Matthew? He was telling several parables to explain what will matter when we get to heaven. Jesus said that we should desire to get to the end of our lives and hear the Master say to us,

> Well done, good and faithful servant! You have been faithful with a few things; I will put you in charge of many things. Come and share your master's happiness! (25:23)

As we begin to put on the words of Jesus from His sermon, we can bring our lives alongside this passage and let God check our progress. If we should long to hear the Father say to us, "Well done, good and faithful servant," then how do our lives line up with those words? Is our offering becoming a beautiful expression of our desire?

Well done. Not well written or well thought or well believed, but well done. We are becoming doers of the Word of God. We are called to act in His name, changing our paths and reordering our lives around His instruction. Are we living the Bible instead of just studying the Bible? Are we becoming women whose lives mirror the active, living, changing power of Jesus?

Good. Our goodness reflects our longing to be in a right relationship with God. Not our perfection in that process, but a deep thirst for right living and intimate fellowship. It is good when we desire to put on the character of Christ and grow in relationship with Him.

Faithful. Are we keeping our eyes fixed on God? Often our faithfulness is proved when things aren't going so well. How are you in the dark? Do you still believe in the God you cannot see? Remember the saying *Where you can see, no faith is required.* Have we been faithful to look toward the Father even in our failings? Our weaknesses? Our regrets? Are you diligent to stay the course?

Servant. We exist to satisfy the Master. We can be directed by His choosing and learn to submit with humility and great joy. We serve from a heart that longs to be like Him. Do we serve Him? Reflect back to Him our gratefulness? Reverence His holiness with our lives?

The Father desires that we would build a house of strong character, firmly established on the foundation of Jesus Christ. The character of a woman that is being changed into the likeness of Christ is a beautiful offering to God. I hope you have heard me over and over: God doesn't require perfection. He realizes that your offering will be bent, chipped, and broken. He delights to show you mercy and grace. He knows that it's just you. He understands that you need a Savior.

But your desire to be like Him is so pleasing. It is good that even in the smallest steps, you keep moving in His direction, that you persevere with God. Romans 5:4–5 says that perseverance produces character and from that character comes hope, and hope in God never disappoints.

The House of Good Deeds

We know that our works cannot save us. They do not make us good enough for God. There is nothing we can do to earn the love or favor of God. It is a free gift, given to any who ask, so that no one can ever boast. But beyond our salvation is the call to build a house of good deeds. We are supposed to weave acts of righteousness into our lives as an offering of worship to our God.

God chose you and me for Himself and made a way for us to fellowship with Him through His Son, Jesus. He calls us beautiful in Psalm 45:11 and pursues us with His passionate love. He wants you and me to know what it's like to dance the dance of our lives in His arms.

God says that we can weave a garment of beauty through our good deeds that readies us for the wedding of the Lamb. Let's take a look at the following verses:

> Then I heard a voice from heaven say, "Write: Blessed are the dead who die in the Lord from now on."
>
> "Yes," says the Spirit, "they will rest from their labor, for *their deeds will follow them*." (Revelation 14:13, emphasis mine)

Have you ever read that before? In the above passage, God says that our deeds follow us into heaven. Wow. Now look at this verse:

> For the wedding of the Lamb has come,
>   and his bride has made herself ready.
> Fine linen, bright and clean,
>   was given her to wear.
> (Fine linen stands for the righteous acts of the saints.)
>   (Revelation 19:7–8)

I promise, I did not add the parentheses in that verse. That's exactly the way it's written in the Bible. The bride of Christ (those who have been saved) is made ready for the celebration wedding of the Lamb by the covering of her righteous acts. Good deeds matter, not only on this earth as an offering to His glory, but also because those deeds follow you into heaven. Your acts of goodness become the beautiful garment that you wear to the wedding of the Lamb.

Some have the idea that we will all receive the same rewards in heaven, but it's just not true. All that believe on Jesus shall be saved, but there will differing rewards in heaven based on the quality of your deeds. Remember these words of Paul:

> But each one should be careful how he builds. For no one can lay any foundation other than the one already laid, which is Jesus Christ. If any man builds on this foundation using gold, silver, costly stones, wood, hay or straw, his work will be shown for what it is, because the Day will bring it to light. It will be revealed with fire, and the fire will test the quality of each man's work. If what he has built survives, he will receive his reward. If it is burned up, he will suffer loss; he himself will be saved, but only as one escaping through the flames. (1 Corinthians 3:10–15)

Can you see the progression of these passages? The building that takes place in your life matters. The materials that you build with matter. Impure motives will be burned away, and the pure deeds that you build on the strong foundation of Jesus will follow you into heaven.

You already know that life is speeding by so quickly, so the message to us is clear: Adjust your life! Live differently! Be good stewards of everything you have been entrusted with. You have been redeemed with a purpose, not only for this earth, but for all eternity. This can't wait any longer. Too much time has already passed. It's time for you and me to begin building on the rock of Jesus, for the glory of God.

You Will Stand

We only get one life to build for the glory of God. That's why the Sermon on the Mount matters. This is why it matters that your life becomes a beautiful offering to God. It matters where and how you build your house, because the life you have built on Jesus is all that will stand. What you have done and created and loved in the name of Jesus is all that will last.

It will stand through the storms you may face on this earth, and it will stand through the judgments of eternity. There is no escaping hardship or difficulties. Trials, testing, sorrows, pain, suffering, disappointment, and death will come to each of us. But everything we build on the strength of Jesus Christ will endure forever.

> *What you have done and created and loved in the name of Jesus is all that will last.*

At the end of His sermon, Jesus was saying to us, *Take this teaching I have just given to you and make it a part of your life. Start slow if you must. But build a life on Me. I am strong. I am the cornerstone. I will not fail you through rain or flood or wind. I am the only way to enter into the happiness of the Master. I am the only foundation that will not give way. Start with Me. Rely on Me. Finish with Me and enter into the eternal celebration of My glory. Everything you build on Me will stand.*

Returning God's Love with Your Life

My offering is meager and tarnished, but oh, how I desire that it become beautiful. Will you run with me toward the arms of our

Father? Will you begin to try on the truth of Jesus' words and let them take hold in your life? Will you let the When You Are's become your blessings? Will you hear Jesus say, *As you go . . . be like Me*, and then respond with your life?

The life that is in front of us can be more beautiful than we could have dreamed. You have more love to return to God than you could have imagined.

A few weeks ago my pastor told of two races on a Saturday. That morning his wife, my friend Beth, ran a 5K through their neighborhood. Brad stood in the driveway with his coffee and cheered on his bride. In the afternoon, their daughter Sarah ran cross-country for her high school. This time the whole family stood at the finish line and cheered her start and her victory. Brad said that at both races, he heard himself yelling for his girls, "Spend it all!"

Life is a journey. Sometimes a race and sometimes a crawl. You can hold back and hesitate. You can live in fear and respond half-heartedly. But would you decide to give everything you have for the glory of God? There is nothing to hoard, because God replenishes so freely. There is no reason to resist or question His love. God has already proved that He's wild about you.

Lift up your eyes this day and fix your gaze on the One who calls you beautiful. Determine in your heart that you will return His love with your life. Decide with your mind to put on the truths of Christ that make your offering beautiful. Do whatever it takes. Spare no expense. Run with the whole of your energies into the arms of your Beloved.

Spend it all, my friend. Spend it all.

Questions for Reflection and Discussion

1. I love that it's never too late to become the woman you have always wanted to be. Maybe you have built on sand in the past, but you can start over. You can build your life on the rock of Jesus. Describe the woman you have always wanted to be.

2. If the whole instruction of Jesus feels like an elephant that you can't swallow, what is the first small bite that you can take? Where can you begin? What is the next right thing?

3. You might be surprised to realize that your righteous deeds are taken with you to heaven. Does that motivate you or discourage you to build a house of good deeds? Why or why not?

4. We've spent a whole book on the idea, but spend a few minutes dreaming about your life as a beautiful offering back to God. Are you ready to begin afresh? Are you assured of God's love and His net of grace?

5. If you decide to "spend it all" for the glory of God, things could get exciting and messy and your life could really change. Are you ready? We only get one of these; I am praying for you right now that more than anything you want to spend it all for God. Is there anything standing in your way?

When Jesus had finished saying these things, the crowds were amazed at his teaching, because he taught as one who had authority. (Matthew 7:28–29)

ACKNOWLEDGMENTS

A FEW YEARS AGO, MY FRIEND JAMIE GAVE ME A LITTLE angel with a lantern. She is called the Angel of Hope. It was the perfect gift given at just the perfect time. I didn't have very much hope back then so I put the angel on the windowsill above my sink, and she became a sweet reminder of the hope I have been prom- ised in Jesus.

Last summer I was raising the blinds in my window and the angel got knocked over and her lantern broke off. I thought, *Great, there goes my hope*. It was a clean break and so I thought I could fix it, you know, superglue that baby back together. I'm not too handy, but I thought surely I could glue. Anybody can glue. For three or four days I tried, and the lantern of hope just kept falling off.

One day my friend Lisa came over and I showed her my angel. I told her my hope was broken and she laughed. "Dave can fix this," she said.

"I don't think it can be fixed, I've tried with two different cement glues," I said, as if I am a crafty girl.

A couple of days later, Lisa brought my angel home. The lantern was securely replaced and hope was restored. It's good to have friends who can fix things.

Sometimes I get to thinking I can do it all by myself. I act as though I can find my own way and fix my own hope, but I can't. God has sent some amazing people into my life, and in these past

213

years they have done what I could not do. They have taken my broken pieces and glued my hope back together and stood beside me acting as if they can't even see the cracks anymore.

My family and friends have given unending support in the writing of this book. They keep the lantern of hope lit for me. They tell me I can when I am sure that I cannot. Thank you for love beyond reason and circumstance.

Thank you to Creative Trust and Nelson Books for running ahead of me and making a way for this message. What a great privilege to work with you all.

And Jesus, I am so grateful. I pray these words are a beautiful offering to You. More than anything, I want to return Your love with my life. Thank You for overcoming every darkness with the brilliant light of Your hope.

About the Author

Angela Thomas is an ordinary woman in passionate pursuit of God, even in the midst of long days of writing, traveling, and packing sack lunches for her four children. She's been honored to walk alongside women of all ages and walks of life through her books and speaking engagements. Angela received her Master's degree from Dallas Theological Seminary. By sharing honestly from her own brokenness, God has given her the tools to minister in the lives of others so powerfully.

For more information on Angela, visit
www.AngelaThomas.com

For information on having Angela speak to your group, please contact:

Creative Trust
(615)297-5010
info@creativetrust.com